MW00398080

Sunrise Ponders

Sandi Hall

ISBN 978-1-63903-056-9 (paperback)
ISBN 978-1-63903-057-6 (digital)

Copyright © 2022 by Sandi Hall

All rights reserved. No part of this publication may be reproduced, distributed, or transmitted in any form or by any means, including photocopying, recording, or other electronic or mechanical methods without the prior written permission of the publisher. For permission requests, solicit the publisher via the address below.

Christian Faith Publishing
832 Park Avenue
Meadville, PA 16335
www.christianfaithpublishing.com

Printed in the United States of America

I dedicate *Sunrise Ponders* to my husband, Barry.

The publishing of this book was a birthday gift from him to me. What he doesn't realize is, "*he*" is my gift.

Barry, thank you for the love, respect, loyalty, safety, humor, stubbornness, and especially the sunrise deck you built for me that ignited so many ponders.

I love you, I do.

Contents

Introduction

Welcome to what goes on in the interior of my brain. Sometimes it is deep, profound, and useful. Sometimes, it is deep, equivocal, and totally unuseful. Almost always, it is deep. I can't help myself... I am a ponderer!

The backyard of our home in Rio Vista, California, faced directly east viewing a small airport with the Sierra Nevadas off in a distance. My husband built me a "sunrise deck" that was tall enough for me to sit, ponder, drink my coffee, pray, watch the sunrise, and meet with God each morning.

This is not a traditional devotional, but my morning ponderings kindled from a "word" stuck in my head. The count of ponderings is not based on days in a year, but the amount of words that stuck in my head. So, if you miss a day, not to worry. I didn't.

My intention is to be honest and authentic about daily struggles as a Christian woman. As Christians, I feel we are so driven to be "like Christ" we forget to let Him mold and sanctify us himself. These ponderings are simply me allowing God to sanctify me, and sometimes me resisting it.

Welcome.

Truth and Schism

Truth: *n.*, conformity to fact or reality; exact accordance with that which is, or has been, or shall be.

Schism: *n.*, a division or separation.

On this first, crisp, early morning of January 2020, I sleepily walked out to the sunrise deck my hubby made for me, hoping to find clouds and color on the new morning sunrise canvas God had created for me to view. This morning I was certain I would find a sparkling, clear sky to represent the new year. What I got was beautiful cloud filled truth.

The truth is, we can spend a day dreaming of a sparkling clear 2020 with no schism involved, but that is just not truth.

The truth is, our 2020 will have clarity, fog, beauty, clouds, joy, and yes, schism.

For me, it will also hold my first grandchild and a sunrise… every morning.

The Truth is, found in the inspired Words of God.

I shall, study, discover and ponder…

Neon Ribbon

Neon: n., a chemical element with the symbol "Ne" and atomic number 10. It is a noble gas. It is also a colorless, odorless, inert monatomic gas under standard conditions, with about two-thirds the density of air.

Good to know there is a "noble gas." Whatever…

I could not capture the true beauty of that neon ribbon in the sky just above the mountains. At first, it was a black ribbon and then within about ten minutes' time, turned to neon orange. Hence, the reason I "searched" the element Ne.

I can't help but think of the verse from Isaiah 61:3, which is so meaningful to me personally.

"To provide for those who grieve in Zion—to give them a crown of beauty for ashes, the oil of joy for mourning, and a garment of praise for a spirit of despair. So they will be called oaks of righteousness, the planting of the LORD, that He may be glorified."

When in ashes, wait for *"the planting of the LORD, that He may be glorified."*

When my "ribbon" is black, I shall wait for He who is "noble" to turn that ribbon into brightness.

I shall ponder…

Gauge

v., to appraise, estimate, or judge.

I always peek outside our bedroom window when I first arise in the early morning darkness. I don't know why; it is generally complete darkness with no hint of the clouds or sunrise to come, yet I peek. What I can see are the street lights outside, which tell me if it's foggy. I can use it as a gauge, which tells me I may want to stay inside just a tad longer than usual.

This morning, I was able to gauge a foggy morning, and I stayed inside just a tad longer than usual.

There was a family conversation around the card table recently, that revealed to my new in-laws that it is not when I speak out that my anger can be gauged, but when I am quiet and retreat. I'm pretty sure there is a "look" that goes with that "silent retreat."

On the other hand, I am generally not a crier, and my emotions cannot be gauged by the lack of an outward sign.

I guess the thing about gauges are—even if absolutely accurate—they last only a moment in time.

In my daughter's teen years, she and her daddy would butt heads, often. While I may have correctly gauged the magnitude of the argument; generally, I horrendously misgauged the "length of time" that magnitude lasted, which annoyed me.

This post is certainly more self-relevant than profound. I am learning that the accuracy of those things I gauge throughout the day—fog, emotions, daily tasks and encounters, etc.—becomes mute if I don't both interpret them correctly and keep the gauge "on."

I shall ponder…

Absolute Infinite

a concept, an extension of the idea of infinity proposed by mathematician Georg Cantor.

There were beautiful thin cloud lines contrasting the sunrise moments before it was hidden by the fog. Lines; a line drawn in the sand, a starting/finishing line, a dance line, lines in geometry, and more.

The thing about lines in geometry are, they either represent the shortest distance between two points or an actual line that can be drawn with little arrow "thingies" on either end to represent a line with both no beginning or end...infinity, so they say.

Enough of the geometry lesson. What intrigues me is the word *infinity*—numberlessness (according to the Dictionary of Sandi). It intrigues me because in a mathematical world of numbers and absolutes there is also allowance for such numberlessness.

Cantor linked the Absolute Infinite with God and believed that it had various mathematical properties, including the reflection principle which is the belief that every property of the Absolute Infinite is also held by some smaller object.

Here we go!

God is the absolute infinite, and His people are His reflection.

Who knew you could get a spiritual lesson from geometry?

I shall ponder...

Wonder

n., the emotion aroused by something awe-inspiring, astounding, or surprising.

It was so clear, still, and cold this morning. I enjoyed watching the fog rise from the pastures. Often, as I look out toward the Sierras, I "wonder"—wonder if there is a group of hikers preparing to make the trek up Half Dome in Yosemite, or a family getting ready for a magnificent breakfast at FireSign Cafe in Lake Tahoe (of course, ordering a California Eggs Benedict), maybe a fisherman or woman throwing out the first flies of the day. I love the Sierras. Always have.

My memories go deep in the Sierras, family camping trips twice a year in my childhood, many backpacking and downhill skiing trips in my twenties, camping in the Redwoods while a flash flood raged through our campsite—eight months pregnant. My daughter learning to ride her bike years later in those same Redwoods. Yes, my memories go deep.

My wonders for the future in those Sierras are countless. My daughter is pregnant with our first grandchild and she and my son-in-law have the same love for those mountains. I certainly wonder if my grandchild (who I am endearingly calling "PO"—Precious One) will have similar adventures and experiences.

Will PO hike to the top of Half Dome? Backpack and snowboard through the mountaintops? Throw a fly out into the rivers that come from those mountaintops? Enjoy California Eggs Benedict at FireSign Cafe? I pray PO does enjoy those passions of mine, but if not, I pray that PO becomes fully who she/he was meant to be and not "expected" to be.

I am blessed…

I shall ponder…

Annoyed

adj., aroused to impatience or anger.

Invariably, each morning when I surface to meet the sunrise, I am met with powerfully spiritual moments that cannot be matched with others in the day. The truth is, this morning I *did* get a powerfully, spiritual, moment, but it was exactly that—"a moment."

The first light in the sky was a curtain of orange over the Sierras. It was magnificent, and there ended my powerfully, spiritual moment.

I noticed in my camera lens a light at the airport drawing the eye to itself rather than the sunrise. While maneuvering my tripod to click an uninterrupted vertical view of the sunrise, a chain reaction evolved that ended in noises waking my next-door neighbor and her dog, Gigi.

Back to the sunrise...that was clearly almost over. Feeling annoyed, I lost sight of the beauty, and was shocked at how easily it happened.

I decided to trek back in to my warm and cozy prayer chair to bring me back to "spiritual reality." Heading down the stairs of my sunrise deck with tripod, camera, coffee, and iPhone in hand; I slipped and fell—boom, boom, boom. Butt sore, but technology and coffee safe.

Passing through the kitchen I noticed my dog Franklyn giving me "the look" that he was trying to tell me something. There, on the floor, was a trail of pooh my other pup, Harriet, had left.

Finally, I see my prayer chair—warm with an electric blanket, several pillows, and the ability to recline... I know my "spiritual moments" are close. Just as I am about to fall into said chair... Franklyn heists his leg for a pee at the bottom of my electric blanket. *Are you kidding me?* Yes, annoyed!

So as I sit here "ranting" about my morning, I ponder back... again, to the moment, that moment, when I realized how easy it was to lose sight of the beauty... If I had only determined to focus back on the presence of the Lord.

I shall ponder...

Cleansed

v., to free from dirt, contamination, or impurities.

Both my internal meter and my husband told me it was a foggy morning. In fact, the hubs said it was the foggiest morning he has experienced so far at our Rio Vista home. I determined to go out… no camera in hand…to meet with the Lord.

The coolness and the wet lightly sprinkled my face. It was refreshing. I looked out and I saw nothing. I heard nothing. Though I couldn't see or hear anything… I could feel…both on my exterior and my interior…the cleansing and refreshing of a new day.

I sat in silence, and just experienced.

It was a while before I asked the Lord what He had for me this morning, and it was okay that I received nothing… I just continued to rest in cool, refreshing, silence and prayed for those I love.

I am cleansed…

I shall ponder…

Turn Around

n., the act or an instance of turning about and facing or moving in the opposite direction.

I knew it was, again, going to be a foggy morning when I grabbed my first cup of coffee at 3:02 a.m. I peeked out and sure enough…it was foggy. Several hours later, I decided to go out anyway. I again enjoyed the cool sprinkle of fog on my face.

I had a deeply needed, both inflecting and "out-flecting," time of prayer. I usually pray with my eyes open (I know…a rebel), but prayer came deepest with my eyes closed this morning. When I opened them… I peered out into the fog…no airport in sight. It made me remember a time when I looked for God, and all I saw was fog.

My remembrance was pulled back twenty-seven years to a time when I had my license pulled due to a seizure, a drug ridden neighbor was warring with us, and I received a phone call that my brother-in-law experienced a severe stroke. As I was packing for our travels to support my sister-in-law and family, our upstairs toilet "broke" and water was slowly flooding our bedroom. At that moment, I remember saying out loud, "Lord, where are you?" followed by "Lord, I am no longer talking to you!"

Well, *that* certainly took care of *that*! Ha!

I tried "not" talking to the Lord… I wasn't very good at it. The fog seemed to last quite a while…months…if not an entire year.

I have since "evolved," and know when I am looking out into the fog, I simply need to "turn around" and look for the Lord where I can find him, creation, scripture, worship, stillness…

I shall ponder…

Rain

n., moisture condensed from the atmosphere that falls visibly in separate drops.

I love the rain…even though it makes the arthritis in my back sing in dissension. I love the sound, the freshness. As a kid-lette, I loved to play in the puddles and I loved my mother for the freedom that allowed me to do so. The fact that it brings fresh water for growth of food and fresh water for our table is incidental….

Recently, I have been praying one aspect of the "fruit of the spirit" each day of the week and am pondering the fruit as a whole on the ninth day. Love, joy, peace, patience, kindness, goodness, faithfulness, gentleness, and self-control (likely out of order).

My precious prayer partner and I had a discussion about understanding the fruit as a whole…not easy…one fruit…many flavors.

I ponder as I listen to the rain on my rooftop this morning. Rain is needed to make fruit grow.

I ask the Lord; What are the visible, separate drops of spiritual rain that makes my spiritual fruit grow? My answer comes. Scripture. One word, one sentence, one chapter, one book at a time. Knowing that each word, sentence, chapter, book evolves into its own one fruit…the inspired Word of God. (Theology of Sandi, wink, wink!)

I shall ponder…

Names

n., a word or a combination of words by which a person, place, or thing is designated, called, or known.

I took a photo of the "wolf moon" last night. Curiosity sent my hubby and I to search where the name came from.

"Wolf moon," according to Space.com, gets its name from Native American tribes, when people would see packs of wolves in the wintertime, howling outside the villages at night.

Names… I am in the beginning stages of a new art "piece" to submit to the Yosemite Renaissance 36 for year 2021. I am inspired to create something that represents the rightness of Yosemite's Curry Village (and others) being restored back to their original, historic names. My memories are tied to the original names, but most importantly it was disrespectful to the history of Yosemite…the MiWok and Ahwahne Tribes who originally represented its name, and of course David and Jennie Curry.

Names… Soon my daughter and son-in-law will be "naming" their new little baby. I can guarantee you it will not be a random name, but a name with meaning…a name that will be woven into memories with its Grandma Sandi.

Names… I think of the names/labels humanity throws out with negative ease: emo/emotional, hyper/energetic, crazy/psycho. Even worse are the names/labels we put on ourselves such as stupid, ugly, fat, worthless, etc. So devouring.

Names… I now consider the importance of names. That when I call one out…it is accurate. A name that cultivates, not devours.

I shall ponder…

Recycling

v., to pass again or process through a series of changes or treatments.

While in the RV driving south along Highway 1, somehow, Barry and I weaved into a conversation about a "recyclable/combustible" McDonalds/Starbucks cup that is being engineered. In true Hall fashion I "Googled" it to get more information.

It is true the two are working together, but we also got some good laughter out of some of the "fake news" and "opinions" out there. People, a combustible cup is *not* going to solve the world's problems, the return of Christ is, but then, *that* is my opinion also.

What is certainly recyclable is the sunrise and sunset that continues to fill the earth, passing through a series of changes, one day at a time…throughout eternity.

I shall ponder…

Waves

~~~~~~

v., a transfer of energy that travels through space or mass.

The sight and sound of the waves added an entirely new dimension to last night's sunset.

My daughter and niece-lette certainly have had their "waves" of morning sickness.

We've been watching *The Crown* on Netflix. The queen certainly does have her "wave" down.

The wave that touches my day most is the wave my mom gives me each morning with her little arthritic ridden hand. It was the same sweet wave she gave to a family friend as she was walked down the aisle at my daughter's wedding.

My mom's simple little wave certainly transfers the energy of love through space and the mass of a heart.

Such a simple tender thing. It really doesn't take much.

I shall ponder...

Always

adv., each and every time.

My morning prayers over the sunrise are generally both as vastly different and simply the same as each sunrise.

Most often the sunrise is reserved for my deepest prayers.

Most often it includes prayer for three dear friends—one who lost a daughter, one who lost a mother and one, recently diagnosed with stage 3 breast cancer. I have lost "ones" dear to me, had a breast cancer scare myself, but have never walked their walk.

Most often my prayer begins by asking the Lord to lead me in prayer for them—from His perspective, not my own.

Most often I am drawn to scripture words that are repeated over and over again in the Old Testament. Words that are but a part of a prescription for God's "hesed." Words such as *love, mercy, kindness,* and more...

Always, God's "hesed" endures forever. These words are true despite my faith, confidence, worries or fears...

"His 'hesed' endures forever."

I shall *ponder*...

Strength and Endurance

Strength: *n.,* the quality of physical power, capacity.
Endurance: *n.,* the ability to withstand hardship or stress.

We "glamped" next to a huge, beautiful, old oak tree. Who doesn't love an old oak tree? Even the most slighted or damaged oak brings its own beauty…standing as its own piece of art. The oak stands for strength and endurance in many cultures. Certainly in my own.

Strength and endurance…they certainly go hand in hand. I have used the two when crossing many a finish line. One, a marathon finish line when I was a younger whipper snapper, but the one I pulled most strength and endurance from was just before my sixtieth birthday when I ran a 5K with my "girls," my daughter and my husband.

The story is much too long. But the short version is: I was injured in 2000 and told I wouldn't "run" again. Fast-forward to 2005, friends who didn't know I was a runner prayed I would "run again"; literally moments later, I got a phone call from my daughter, saying, "Mom, you may think I'm crazy, but I believe you're going to run again"…uhhh huhhhh…crazy! Fast-forward…2016 (is there such a thing as "slow," fast-forward…anyway) I crossed that 5K finish line enfolded in the arms of my daughter and hubby.

I guarantee you, the sixteen years of preceding strength and endurance work it took to get me across that finishing line was not pretty…especially the sweat left on the gym floor. I didn't do that work because I believed I would "run again," but because I am an oak tree, full of strength and endurance, damaged, but standing as its own piece of art.

I shall ponder…

Sociology

n., the study of human behavior.

Yesterday we visited an area in San Simeon where the elephant seals live a complete lesson in sociology: birth, rallying of life amongst the seals and sadly, death as well. I would have loved to have brought my chair, coffee, and spent the entire day.

I suppose I wanted to spend the day viewing them because their sociology is not much different from my own; rallying for what I believe is mine…rallying against what I do not want to share with others…the deep, innate need to protect my young ones. Who wouldn't want to spend a vacation cuddling on the beach, listening to the waves crash back and forth while watching sunrise after sunset again and again…

I took over two hundred photos, keeping only about thirty. Most of the photos I kept captured those lessons they were offering in sociology. A few were no more than simply precious.

It reminds me that in the midst of my "sociology," sometimes, I just need to stop and be precious.

I shall ponder…

American

n., of or relating to the United States of America or its people, language, or culture.

I am thankful to be an American…really thankful.

I am thankful to have the ability to roam this country at my own free will.

I am exceedingly thankful for the ability to pray in public, for certainly, I would have been tarred, feathered, and hung at gunpoint by now.

I am thankful to be able to express myself in written and artistic form—even if it is not the opinion of the reader/viewer.

I am thankful for diversity…especially when it breeds unity.

I am thankful to have the right to vote and I take it seriously.

I am especially thankful to the men and women who have fought to protect this country and its freedoms.

There is so much more to be thankful for…

I shall ponder…

Monotony

n., tediously repetitious or lacking in variety.

This morning, the sunrise seemed monochromatic to me…fog, dark clouds, almost complete inability to see where one cloud ended and the other began. This monotony inspired me to do what I had always wanted to do—try my photography skills in black and white. It didn't turn out. It was even more monotonous than real time.

I wonder, when things seem monotonous to me—the same, lacking joy—am I paying attention to what else is around me? That which is not monotonous. Am I willing to find and experience joy in what "is" around me or am I determined to be in my mood of monotony?

I shall ponder…

Flu

n., any of various viral infections, esp. a respiratory or intestinal infection.

The flu...the only time I seem to get it are those years that I take the flu shot. Hmmmm.

I had a Sheldon Cooper experience at the DMV yesterday. I did not seem to have "the number" required for my online, "real ID," preapplication. "No worries," I was told by the DMV rep, there was a computer against a wall at DMV to reapply (and then restand in line I might add).

The first computer I went to creeped me out so much I couldn't help but picture germs overcoming my entire body...lol. I stopped mid-application process and moved to another computer. For whatever reason...that computer didn't creep me out as much.

Application, check!

Application #, check!

DMV "real" ID, check!

Flu, check!

Moral to this story: Make sure you have the "real ID," preapplication "number" before you enter through the DMV doorway.

I may have the flu, but I am now able to roam North America, planes, and federal buildings freely!

No need to ponder, I will just rest...

Beauty

n., the quality present in a person or thing that gives intense aesthetic pleasure or deep satisfaction to the mind or the senses.

These sunrises…this beauty…are not random. They have a purpose.

Romans 1:20 tells me that God's invisible attributes are clearly seen through the creation of the world. Even still… I can't help but perceive that God has created me uniquely, to be in exceptional wonder of this beauty.

Literally, I can sit and just notice the variance of colors and brush strokes—each morning, each day, day after day, visible in the clouds at sunrise. (BTW: I am sure it is also true at sunset, but my deck faces east.)

This wonder is so much so that sometimes it interrupts my prayer time. I believe God's okay with that.

I shall notice and I shall ponder.

Squinting

v., to look with the eyes partly closed, as in bright sunlight.

Being in the last stages of the flu... I sent the hubby out to check on the sunrise for me. He replied back that it was dark, cloudy, and foggy with only two tiny horizontal slits of orange sunrise peeking through. He said it looked like someone was looking through their eyes by squinting. I had no idea what I was *really* going to find out on the deck, but sure enough it looked like someone squinting to see me.

This speaks to me spiritually...sometimes when I am in darkness, and I try to focus on Christ, the Light, it is just too much for me to take in. It's just too bright. Those times that I grab my Bible and flip through the scriptures and just can't seem to find anything that relates to my personal moment in time. It is easy to just put the Bible down in frustration. Maybe, what I am forgetting to do is "squint."

Squinting the Scriptures (Theology of Sandi), when the Bible just seems too big and my "omni" God seems a bit unreachable... I need to "squint the scriptures": shut my eyes (and brain) to what I don't know and focus on what I do know.

I know that God is sovereign...

Within that He is love...

Within that He is good (despite what I both do and don't know).

My "squinting prayer" would be to "rest in His mercy and grace"...

I shall ponder...

Rearview Mirror

n., a mirror on a motor vehicle enabling the driver to see traffic coming behind him or her.

There is not only an airport behind our backyard, but a road as well, Airport Road. Often when I am watching the sunrise I wonder if the cars/trucks coming toward me are checking out the sunrise in their rearview mirrors. I'm tempted to make a lighted sign that says, "Look behind you!"

It's interesting how we have a propensity to look forward for beauty. However, sometimes we need to look backward, in that rearview mirror to see the beauty.

I look backward and think of my friends who have lost loved ones within the last year and realize their only chance to see the beauty of that loved one is to look back in remembrance...often covered with pain. I pray for the process of grief and the Lord's healing to remove that pain...bit by bit.

I look back at the engagements and weddings in my family this last year. Their remembrance is covered with joy. I pray that we all remember that joy comes from the Lord...not an event or fortuitousness.

I look back at the trials of this last year and though they were temporarily covered in hardship...the beauty of a better me has shown through.

I look back at our travels to visit family this last year and understand more deeply the feeling of warmth that comes from the sunrise...though distant. I am thankful for that warmth.

I determine to look in that rearview mirror to see those things of beauty that bring true joy to me, and to the Lord, and to not focus on the trash in the road.

I shall ponder...

Sometimes

adv., from time to time; occasionally.

In 2006, I took a photo of an old oak tree on a dear friend's Iowa property, and used it as inspiration for an art piece I made for her.

It seemed this tree would stand forever, but it didn't.

At the very same time, another tree—not an oak, weak and frail—stood on the opposing end of the same Iowa property. It was suggested many times that this tree should be removed because it was so weak and frail. But its owner denied…determining that she would see it through to strength and life, and she did.

Sometimes that is what we have to do…let an old, strong thing go and sometimes…determine to allow a new, weak thing to grow.

One thing I do know for certain…the strength and endurance of an old oak does not match that of a precious friendship…

I shall ponder…

Warning

n., advice to be cautious.

I *knew* it was going to be a beautiful sunrise. Having checked my "meter," there was not a hint of fog on the horizon. I could see shadows of stark colors over the fence line.

Upon heading outside with a joyful step… I received a "warning." Turns out it is "mating season" for opossums and skunks. *Really!* Please take your necessary reproductive actions elsewhere!

As I stepped on the deck… I was not disappointed with what was going to be a beautiful sunrise. It was still dark-ish, allowing me to watch it unfold.

A tad later, Barry came out to share the sunrise with me. The first thing he noticed was "the warning."

Sooooo interesting… I could no longer smell it. It had become normalcy in such a short time.

That's the thing about "warnings"; they are temporary, and if we don't heed to the thing they are warning us about that very thing becomes a part of our normalcy.

In California, we seem to have warning labels upon entering any establishment, eating any food, watching any movie, etc. A sad truth in California is; the warnings themselves have become perfunctory.

Determining which warning signs are important, and responding to them is necessary.

When I see that warning sign of both "a look" on the face and "vein" in the neck of my hubby when I am performing my blatant form of communication… I know the hard and right thing is to slow down and calm the emotion of my words…knowing I must draw extra caution to ensure those warning signs do not become "normalcy."

I shall ponder…

Decisions

~~~~~~

n., a conclusion or judgment reached after consideration.

Patience brought me the most beautiful sunrise this morning. Usually, the sunrise seems most beautiful early, before it actually rises, when it brings stark contrast in colors. But this morning, as I watched the fog begin to rise toward the sun…the soft golden colors against a Brittany Blue sky were almost ethereal. It took only about seven to eight minutes before the entire sunrise was swallowed up by that fog.

It is so easy to be swallowed up by fog. It can happen in minutes, losing the clarity that was once had. I seem to get caught up in fog when I am trying to make a decision that is not yet meant to be made. (Don't keep me from my decision-making!)

The "waiting" seems to cause me to create my own fog—you know, the perpetual "if this, then that" on and on and on, kind of thing. Making thousands of decisions inside my head while waiting to make one decision outside of it. As I write this, I realize that the fog also comes when I know the right decision, and I do not want to "heed to it."

The thing is (there's always a "thing"), fog is just water droplets—droplets that catch my attention and remind me to stand still and refocus for clarity.

Clarity reminds me; the decision is the Lord's…

I shall ponder…

Perfectionism

n., a propensity for being displeased with anything that is not perfect or does not meet extremely high standards.

This morning, I watched Canadian geese rise in a nondescript grouping and circle above their nighttime resting pond maybe ten times before they mastered their "V" pattern and headed off squawking in the high sky. It was the first time I noticed such a thing... certainly the first time I was able to capture it in digital video format.

I am a perfectionist. If I were a Canadian goose, I could lead that grouping into a "V" pattern in no time! However, as a human, my perfectionism holds me back in artistic creativity. Spiritually speaking, perfection was crucified on the cross...the "imperfect" watched, heard, or read of its happening and the only thing left to do was "believe."

I do believe, however, that perfection can be found in the faith that Christ provides us. Sometimes it is a mustard seed amount of faith, and sometimes it is a mountain full of faith, but it is always perfect. (Theology of Sandi)

The thing is, my obedience, my walk to glorify Christ, and even my comprehension of who Christ is, is imperfect. Christ has accepted that in me and loves me anyway, knowing that I will understand His full truth—one day, on the other side...

I shall ponder...

Big Bang

n., any sudden forceful beginning or radical change.

This morning, the songs of the "after" sunrise were beautiful. I stood motionless on the sunrise deck, enjoying the songs of the birds, geese, chickens, and cows. Unexpectedly, there came a *bang, bang*!

The minutes following were me trying to find Barry to share what I heard. In my head…with a "no fire" zone behind us at the airport… I was sure a human had been shot. Barry explained it was probably in the area behind the airport and the fog kept the sound low, and loud.

The thing about a "bang" in life is that it can be unexpected, unwanted, life changing. One moment everything is fine…life is still and peaceful…the birds are singing, and then bang…nothing is ever the same again. It can come in the form of death, disability, or any loss that causes grief.

The bang creates our turn to display the joy of the Lord through the midst of trial…instead of hearing or reading it from someone else.

My Big Bang Theory (Theology of Sandi) has nothing to do with creation; it is given at a personal level…the bang happens; within it, God awakens us, works a purpose through it, preserves our faith, and "nothing is ever the same again."

I shall ponder…

Reflection

n., an indirect expression, manifestation, or result.

There are no words to describe this morning's sunrise. I generally try to limit my photos to "2" so I am not viewing the sunrise from behind a camera lens. *That* did not happen this morning.

That teeny, tiny prickle of sunlight reflected all of that beauty… both before and after it began its course in the sky. Crazy!

What is even crazier is that Christ has called Christians to the task of reflecting His glory. We all have bad and good, days and moments, reflecting that task.

Sometimes, we hold tightly to a black cloud that surrounds us and reflective light can barely be seen.

Sometimes, we can release ourselves from that black cloud… allowing greater beauty to be seen reflecting from it.

Sometimes, we are out in the open allowing the sun to reflect color and majesty without regard.

I believe I reflect Christ (or not) through what I think: "*Finally, brothers, whatever is true, whatever is honorable, whatever is just, whatever is pure, whatever is lovely, whatever is commendable, if there is any excellence, if there is anything worthy of praise, think about these things*" (Phil. 4:8).

Through what I *say*: "*The good person out of the good treasure of his heart produces good, and the evil person out of his evil treasure produces evil, for out of the abundance of the heart his mouth speaks*" (Luke 6:45).

Through what I do: "*Whatever you do, work heartily, as for the Lord and not for men, knowing that from the Lord you will receive the inheritance as your reward. You are serving the Lord Christ*" (Col. 3:23–24).

Likely, what I "think" is probably where I need to put most of my focus since it is reasonably the catalyst for what I say and do.

Too, too, much to ponder here, but…

I shall ponder…

Cold and Soft

Cold: *adj.,* having a low temperature.
Soft: *adj.,* not sharply drawn or delineated.

The sunrise was "soft" this morning. As the moments grew on…my hands grew colder…even the outside of my Yeti was cold to the touch. Despite the cold…my coffee remained wonderfully warm. Despite the cold…the sunrise became softer still.

Before coming out this morning I was reading/studying in 1 Kings, the accounts where the Kings were provoking God to anger.

I had written in my Prayer Bible, "Lord, what do I do that provokes you to anger?"

As I sit here in this "softness," I can't help but "ponder" the "cold" harshness of some of my "hard" words. I am direct. I say what I think; sometimes what I say is "spiritual," filled with the fruit of the spirit; sometimes what I say is harsh, selfish, and unkind. I am sure this is true to everyone of various degrees, but I am brought back to my original question.

"Lord, what do I say…what do I do…that provokes you to anger?"

I shall ponder…

Go

v., to move on a course; proceed forward.

The geese were out this morning doing their "thing." I tried to figure out what that "thing" was. The cloudless sky gave greater clarity as I watched them move back and forth in some sort of dance.

It seems (Theology of Sandi), there may be resident geese at the pond-o-minium behind our house…offering a Land B&B for those geese that are just passing through. The resident geese help the visitors get up into the air and take the front, more strenuous position, until the visitors are ready to take over and move on. The resident geese then take a break at the pond-o-minium and later meander over to the golf course ponds for a relaxing day.

Going far or going near… I guess we are all called to "go." Maybe to a golf course…maybe a new destination…maybe to work…maybe to the park with our children…maybe it is time to go "far" from a past hurt or away from disappointment that is being held on to. Maybe a habit that binds me from being my best self. Certainly, the Bible tells believers to "go" and preach the Gospel of Christ.

The thing is, sometimes I am called to take a step of faith forward on an unknown course. I am good with that, "except" when I need to "go" on a course I am insecure with. (I mean, who doesn't fear failure?).

I am a woman of great faith, so when my faith is shaken, I forget it is okay to have that mustard seed amount of faith, which can be added to moment by moment and day by day…

The truth is, I have precious "peeps" surrounding me who will walk forward with me on that unknown course…taking the front, strenuous position of prayer and intercession…until I am able to move on in strength and faith.

The truth is, I am blessed.

I shall ponder…

Color

~~~~~~

n., the appearance of objects or light sources described in terms of the individual's perception of them, involving hue, lightness, and saturation.

I love color. Color is simply a perception of names...while at the same time...a marvelously, powerful tool that can create tremendous expressive qualities. This speaks to both my left, scientific and right, creative brain. The interesting thing is, I use the left, scientific side of my brain as a tool for whatever my right brain has for me to create with fabrics. Contrary to normal belief... I do not believe I have a dominant side.

I seem to have surrounded myself with either *very* literal or *very* expressive thinkers. (All or nothing for me!) The interesting thing is when they get into a room with each other their "perceptions" are very different.

What the Theology of Sandi means is, if I were asked to pick a color in the clouds and describe it expressively...likely, I would describe it with intuitiveness, body language, thoughts, and emotions...not literal accuracy. On the other hand, if I were asked to describe one of those colors with the scientific side of my brain, and in fact, I chose one, my answer would be and is #b6, 64, 4e or FF6666.

The thing is, we are all expressive or literal to a certain degree. When working from the literal side of my brain, I need to be patient while listening to an expressive and allow their color to brighten my perception.

On the other hand, when working from the expressive side of my brain I need to understand the impatience of a literal and allow them to bring me back to solid reality.

The two are not opposites, but tools for each other.

Again, I love color, so I shall ponder...

Deeds

n., something that is carried out; an action.

I was pondering which photo to post to my blog this morning…the first sunlight photo was mysterious and beautiful, the sunrise photo was startling and brilliant…then, Barry sent me a video he took for a young man who was sitting by the Rio Vista bridge watching the sunrise. The young man had a flip phone and couldn't get a good photo, so asked Barry to send him the one he took. Such a simple, yet meaningful deed.

Yesterday, we went to our favorite Rio hangout, Pizza Factory, for their salad bar and pizza lunch. A man from Shea Company had paid for more lunches than employees who were able to make their meeting. He saw my mom sitting at a table and gifted us payment for two salad bars. Barry had already paid for our lunch, so we were able to gift the next couple who came in the door. It was also a simple, yet meaningful deed.

How simple it is to do a meaningful deed…a conscious, transference of goodness.

I made split pea soup for my daughter when she was having morning sickness…in return she sent me tortilla soup when I had the flu. We are taking my mom to "chase the sunset" tonight (she is unable to climb up the sunrise deck)—a simple yet *very* meaningful deed for her.

Sometimes a meaningful deed is simply being patient and kind…

I shall ponder…

Fire

~~~~~~

n., the rapid oxidation of a material in the exothermic chemical process of combustion, releasing heat, light, and various reaction products.

The definition "*according to Sandi*" *is* "matter that creates heat and light."

This morning's sunrise brought to mind the word "fire."

Spiritually speaking, I know that God is an all-consuming fire. I know He uses that fire to show His power, His glory and to give light. I know He uses light to symbolize faith and holiness in scripture. I know I am to let my light shine before others. I know for certain God is light, and darkness cannot overcome The Light.

My conclusion is, I am called to "fan into flame the gift of God," to literally rekindle or revive the spark, for if I don't feed the fire, the flame will die down, and I inevitably will find myself standing in darkness…

I shall ponder…

Football

n., a game played by two teams of eleven players each on a rectangular, one-hundred-yard-long field with goal lines and goalposts at either end, the object being to gain possession of a ball and advance it in running or passing plays across the opponent's goal line or kick it through the air between the opponent's goalposts.

Today is the Super Bowl. Yes, I shall root for the 49ers win! I suppose I am rooting more in honor of my father…a die-hard 9'er fan. The thing is… I still don't know how to or when to "root." Even after my induction into, and in-depth study of the game of Fantasy Football… I do not understand what is happening on the field. (BTW: I came in dead last in FFB and won the "crap award.")

One of the things I *don't understand*, why is there a lineup of "dudes" one-on-one against each other so a few another dudes can throw and catch a ball.

Newsflash: Remove the one-on-one dudes and just "offensively" have a thrower and catcher on the field with a couple of those "defensive" players. (I know it's possible because I saw it done on an episode of *Friends*.) It seems it would eliminate the unending amount of injuries and rules.

And another thing, why, why, *why*; when one of the defensive dudes is able to get the ball thrower or catcher on the ground, do a gaggle of 250-plus-pound other "dudes" need to fall in a heap on top of him? I get why a few need to hold him down, but an entire team? Like where do you think the guy underneath is going? Has there ever been an incident where a ball catcher has done a turtle crawl across a "fake" TV line or real end line with a team of defensive players on his back? Doubtful.

Also, why do they call it football? Certainly not because of the percentage of time the ball hits a foot…just sayin'.

What I do understand… I know you think it is nothing, but I do understand getting the ball across the goal line and within those two tall poles.

Tailgating parties, whether at the stadium or in the home bring food and fellowship.

Rooting for the 49ers...wherever/whenever they are on the field, brings me close to my dad and I am proudly wearing his 49'er hat today.

I shall not ponder...

Clarity Interruptus

Clarity: *n.*, clearness of appearance.
Interruptus: *adj.,* broken in conformity; discontinuance.

I was up extra early this morning. I completed morning prayer, study, and devotion before the first sunlight even appeared.

Since the sky seemed so clear, I decided to take my laptop outside to "ponder" in written form right in those elements that bring me so much brain activity.

I imagined myself having more profoundness than even my hard drive could hold.

But *not*! *Waaaay* too cold, even in California! My fingers shivered on the wrong keys. I pulled them into my two layers of robe. My focus was to get back to that keyboard…though the beauty of a clear sky sunrise was about to be before me. The keyboard distraction brought "clarity interruptus."

Once back inside "clarity interruptus" continued… It was okay… I posted my morning blog photo and began my day…lesson learned.

I shall ponder tomorrow…

Fear

n., a very unpleasant or disturbing feeling caused by the presence or imminence of danger.

This morning in my time of scripture prayer for PO ("precious one"), I went to Psalm 56:3 and 4, which basically is David saying to the Lord… When I am afraid, I put my trust in you. I pondered on those things that children fear: the dark, the dentist, rollercoasters, failure, the unknown, being bullied, being lost or left alone, being hurt in a relationship, disappointing parents. I prayed that PO would put his/her trust in the Lord in each instance.

I realized us "adults" still fear in the same things but with a mature twist.

The dark: unable to see far enough ahead to make "intelligible" decisions.

The dentist: every sense is heightened in that dentist chair, young or old.

Rollercoasters of life.

Failure: causing us to *not* try.

Being bullied: by those who want to get us down.

Being lost or left alone: without the support of a committed relationship.

Being hurt while in a relationship: to the point of not wanting to be in one or not knowing how to get out.

Disappointing our parents, our employers, our family, our friends, ourselves?

The thing is, all of these things offer us opportunity. Opportunity to trust in the Lord. Opportunity to know what the "action" actually is, the action of trusting in Him…giving up that fear…falling backward into His arms.

I shall ponder…

Rest

n., a bodily state characterized by minimal functional and metabolic activities.

Such a beautiful morning. The sun rose in such a pure, peaceful, restful, and deeply worshipful way. No words came… I just rested in the moment.

Sometimes that's all I'm supposed to do…rest in the moment.

I shall rest, and I shall ponder…

Choice

n., the power to choose among a variety.

There is a light pole on the road immediately behind my sunrise deck. I usually take my photos from either side. Occasionally, I have learned to just make it a part of the picture.

So many things hit us head on in life…not necessarily bad, not necessarily good, but certainly head on.

My back injury in 2000 definitely created a "being of pain" that hit me head on…even to this day. It took me awhile to not allow it to be the focus of my attention, but to move it aside, allowing me to view the beautiful picture I still had before me.

Certainly, not all days and moments am I able to do this. Admittedly, when I do…it is often with the same frustration I have while looking at that light pole…head-on, that is obstructing my view. However, I am able to do it, and the more I push such things aside…the easier it gets.

The thing is, my perceptual vision is actually a "choice" of how I want to view my picture…my day.

I have a choice to push large "beings" and especially small annoyances to the side so I can see and live my fullest life.

I shall ponder…

Contrast

v. tr., to set in opposition in order to show or emphasize differences.

I have a fascination with opposites. Opposites are easy because they are the absolute contrary to another thing. Contrast simply distinguishes a difference between two things. The opposite of green is red...while the contrast of green is another green...a difference in lightness, darkness, or hue.

Yesterday, I spent hours working on "trees" for a Yosemite Renaissance piece I am working on. The contrast of one tree branch to another, the contrast of one tree to another became daunting... especially when working with only fabrics from silk ties and cotton colors available in my "stash."

This morning I read Psalm 2. It mentions in verse 11...to serve the Lord with fear and rejoice with trembling.

Fear, according to Sandi, "simplified," is reverence to God's sovereignty.

At first glance, fear and joy seem like opposites, and rejoice and trembling seem like opposites.

While viewing the sunrise, and its "contrasts," I wondered if fear, joy, and trembling are all contrasts of one another. Distinguishing differences in each other but all explicably part of the same picture.

Spiritually speaking, either joy or fear without a contrasting counterpart could put us in a place the Lord would not choose us to be. Scripture calls us to dance in the Lord... *Dance*, but dance in a way that expresses rejoicing in the Lord, while "fear without joy is torment" (W. L. Watkinson).

I shall ponder...

Whisper

n., to speak softly with little or no vibration of the vocal cords, especially to avoid being overheard.

I am writing "before" the sunrise…listening to the harsh wind blow outside…knowing I will go outside to meet the sunrise, but not for an extended stay.

Earlier this morning (yes, there is an "earlier" to my "early"), as I was listening to the winds rage… I was praying for God's specific direction in a path He seems to be leading Barry and I on.

I randomly came across a scripture prayer in my journal Bible. Well, I guess not so random. It was where the little, thin, silk bookmarker was placed in 1 Kings 19 in my Bible. My eye was drawn to one of my scripture prayer notations. I barely remember writing it, but its profoundness to where I am right now in life was startling. May I be so bold as to share?

"Lord, You are preparing me to hear your whisper. May I be so patient and faithful to hear your voice in a whisper and to not require the force of wind, earthquake, or fire. Lord, may I be patient in spite of those forces to hear you in a whisper, to not analyze what the forces of nature may be saying—but to know it is time to listen and wait for your force, given in a whisper."

I shall ponder…. Again…

Calm

adj., nearly or completely motionless; undisturbed.

Such an unbelievably "calm" sunrise after a day of unimaginable windstorms.

My fascination with opposites continues. I am always taken by opposites represented in scripture: Life/Death, Light/Dark, Good/Evil, Love/Hate, Victory/Persecution, Fruitfulness/Pruning, Blessed/Cursed. Just a few of the opposites I have logged in the front of my Bible.

Without one, we would not understand the other.

Wind/Calm...

The Bible speaks of a wind that goes where it wishes and also a wind that reveals the Holy Spirit... God's expression of Himself to us.

Calmness, however, is what we are to express back to God.

Can I express a calmness back to the Lord as true as His power in and through the wind?

I shall ponder...

Illusions

n., an erroneous perception of reality.

Last night the moon seemed especially huge. Barry and I saw it rising over the horizon, and though I didn't have the proper lenses... I had to snap a few photos anyway. I know the moon is always the same size, but sometimes it just doesn't seem so. I believe it is called an "illusion." In fact, there is even a "thing" called the "moon illusion."

An erroneous perception of reality...

So many directions to go here.

Intentions? Affections? Wealth? Time? Strength? Weakness? Knowledge? How about we turn presidential debates into a Jeopardy game show...just sayin'...no illusions there...

Magic shows are dependent on illusions. We know it's true, but we just can't figure some of them out.

Our humanness can bring an illusion that wrongly represents Christianity to the rest of the world, and with even greater sadness, within the family of God itself. You know...wanting to be perceived more "Christlike" than we really are. Afraid to share our true self.

The thing is: wouldn't the lack of "spiritual" illusion cause our actual spiritual growth to be stronger and healthier?

Illusions seem to be for the benefit of man...while "truth" is of benefit to both man and God.

I shall ponder...

Book Club

n., a group of people who meet to discuss the books they have been reading.

I love Tuesday mornings. It's the time my prayer partner and I meet. I don't want it to be misinterpreted that we spend two hours in intercession. But it is a special time that I don't otherwise have in my week. A time when we weave back and forth what is on our hearts and weave back and forth...prayer, which inevitably takes us somewhere profound. A "somewhere" we can ponder on until we meet the next week.

We have been meeting together for thirteen years now.

It all started as a "closed" book club. (I laugh... I don't believe we made it through any one book...though we certainly tried). There were four founding members...one by one...the "host" of the book club moved away... Santa Cruz, California... Arizona... Rio Vista, California, and soon...the last one to Arizona.

It seems the moral of this ponder may be to not host a book club unless you are open to a "move." (Hey! My first prayer partner moved away also to Iowa...what's up with that?)

I can't let this group of women go unmentioned. God used these women to challenge me when I wanted to be "right," encourage me when I was down, love me when I was and wasn't unlovable, and profoundly change me into a better woman of God.

I propose we have a California meets Arizona summit once each year...get the whole group back together, and hey...maybe we should all read the same book before we meet!

I shall be encouraged...

I shall ponder...

Exhaust

n., the waste gas from an engine or the pipe the gas flows through.

There was an abnormal amount of "exhaust" lines in the sunrise this morning.

That sky perfectly defined me this morning. I had a sleepless night, which led to *waaaaay* too much pondering. Thoughts going in so many directions…leaving a trail of exhaust behind my eyes.

You see, Barry and I have decided to put our Rio Vista home up for sale to move closer to Kaiser Medical (forty minutes away) and of course the secondary benefit of being closer to Brad, Elise, and our new little PO due in a handful of months.

As I sat and pondered on all of those exhaust lines… I quietly… even peacefully asked the Lord to direct our path.

When I came inside, I opened my Bible to Psalm 5 to write a scripture prayer for PO, and there it was in verse 8, David was asking the Lord to: "*Make your way straight before my face.*" David didn't ask the Lord to make his own way straight, but to make the Lord's way straight before him.

How much easier is it to walk God's path before me…step by step…than to continuously be crying out for God to straighten the constantly sidetracked wanderings of my own path?

I shall ponder…

Opportunity

n., a favorable or advantageous circumstance or combination of circumstances.

I spent a loooong time out on the sunrise deck this morning in the California cold. I could see the Sierras topped deeply with snow. The cloud art above them was beautiful, but the photo I chose to shoot this morning was the actual sun beginning to rise over my cow friends further east. They are rarely over in that particular pasture so I took the opportunity to a grab digital memory of them.

Opportunity…it can be hard to grab when it strikes.

Personally, I love opportunity. In my fifties and earlier, I used to embrace change, but now, I embrace opportunity, because I can take it or leave it.

My hubby has mentioned I have become less "embracive" of opportunities lately. I feel no need to analyze why.

But after pondering, I do feel the need to push myself through more opportunity, because the thing is, you *can* take it or leave it, but you can also lose it.

What opportunity can I grab hold of today?

I shall ponder…

Garments

n., a covering.

Each winter morning, I put on two pink robes and a pair of Ugg's before I go out to the deck. Sometimes I add on my sweats or a rain coat. Cozy.

I started pondering about the garments we are to layer on in Christ...garments of compassion, kindness, humbleness, patience, love (Colossians 3).

In contrast, I thought about Lazarus who had been raised from the dead and Jesus told Lazarus to take off the grave clothes. Though I am sure the call may have had something to do with the horrendous smell of death Lazarus was "literally" carrying around with him... I am also sure there is an allegorical, spiritual meaning of greater importance.

Death clothes: unforgiveness, resentment, deceit...

What if, I figuratively "called out" and took off my grave clothes each night? Those things I layered on during the day that displayed death instead of life? I will be transparent in saying that I have been carrying around resentment and stubbornness. What if I didn't spend my time explaining to God why I deserve to have those garments on, but simply took them off?

What if... I figuratively put on the garments Christ calls me to layer on in my life with Him each morning? What if I planned and determined to show compassion, kindness, humbleness, patience, and love in very specific situations throughout my day? What if...

I shall ponder...

Stuff

n., the tangible substance that goes into the makeup of a physical object.

I started staging our home for an upcoming open house. Packing up books, Bible reference tools, wall art, and "stuff" we just couldn't pass up at Hobby Lobby. Other than several pieces of original art... the walls look bare, but clean.

One could ask, do I really need this stuff that became the makeup of my home? Wellllll, after much pondering, this "one" would answer, to some extent, yes, and to some extent, no.

I suppose I could let go of some of my old and dusty Bible reference books that I now use the internet for, but they do remind me of a time...before the internet...when I devoted my life to Christ, and studied relentlessly to "know Him."

I could get rid of some of the Hobby Lobby "words" I have, but the words especially remind me to "be still" and "pray big."

Stuff is hard to get rid of. It can lose its originally intended purpose and become a piece of memory or sentiment, *or* it can be "stuff with potential," case in point, my art room. Soooo much potential lies within those walls!

After much pondering... I am keeping one reference book. It is the first one I bought, an exhaustive concordance for sentiment's sake. I was able to weed down my books on prayer from ten to seven (those three, I was "pained" by the authors view on prayer anyway!). I am keeping the words because...well, I love words and they point me to Christ.

The ponder...other than how I am going to start packing up my art room today...well, I am not sure there is a ponder...

Likely, I will ponder anyway...

One Step

n., a ballroom dance consisting of a series of unbroken rapid steps in 2/4 time.

There is a treacherousness of putting our home of only two years up for sale...of not knowing where I will land. But if I only take it one step further...render faith in knowing God will land me where He wants me/us to be. *That* is where peace will be found. It's that next step that is (as my grandpa would say) a doozey! Why is that I ask?! Wouldn't I be relentless in that next step...knowing peace is on the other side?

Well, as I ponder, I realize it is because I want to know the "whole" picture, not just the next step. Planning is good—necessary—it falls under the realm of wisdom, but equally as often my steps in the Christian world are called to be of faith and obedience. Personally, I prefer wisdom. Whatever...

This reminds me of a previous post realizing I should be walking God's path, and not asking him to constantly be redirecting my own. My question is, how do I do that?

Which brings me back to "one step at a time." Focus on the step I am to take next, *now*, not the stepping blocks down the road.

My next dance step is to make my art room presentable (I did throw away three old spools of thread yesterday!).

With three average and one large mid-arm sewing machine, loads of precious threads, bushels of silk ties, heaps of cotton stash, and treasures of wood, shells, feathers, and such, the task is daunting. The organization I thrive on in the "real" world, oddly, can't be found in my creative space.

However, as the sun rises "one step at a time," so shall I—in wisdom, obedience, and faith.

I shall ponder...

Hesed

A *working definition* is "a love demonstrated through the life and death of our Savior Jesus Christ."

It was praise time out on the ol' deck this morning. This song kept running through my mind, so I just began to sing it out into the sunrise (I "think" my neighbor is on vacation again… Right!?).

"The steadfast love of the Lord never ceases. Your mercies never come to an end; they are new every morning, new every morning, great is your faithfulness, O Lord, great is your faithfulness!"

I am drawn to the word "steadfast" love…"*hesed*" love. I have been reading a book and attending a discussion study from the book by Michael Card, *Inexpressible*. The book digs into the word "hesed." It takes a book to begin to understand the word because there is actually no English translation. (Merriam-Webster concurred).

Michael wrote, "Understanding hesed is a lifelong journey." In a margin of the book, I wrote, "the consistent, ever-faithful, relentless, constantly-pursuing, lavish, extravagant, unrestrained, furious love of our Father God, and that's just the start!"

I shall ponder…

Cropping

v., the removal of unwanted outer areas from a photographic or illustrated image.

Sometimes it's hard to know where to crop a photo. What is seen in any sunrise photo is only a glimpse of the entire sighting. Any cropping eliminates a portion of the "whole" view. However, comma, without cropping…the photo would lack some of the details I see.

For example: this morning I took a sunrise photo which included nine dots of barely seen geese flying in the distance. A good shot of those geese would have required quite a bit of cropping and the loss of several soft, large, puffy, pink, and white clouds in a vastness of distance that was incomprehensible.

I am slowly, but surely, doing an inductive study through the Bible. I am currently one year in to the study and almost through 2 Kings. If I look at the task in a complete view of accomplishment…it can be overwhelming and seemingly unending. But if I take it chapter by chapter, verse by verse… I am focusing exactly on the study of the day, and making forward progress.

On the other hand, any chapter/verse I am studying *must* be taken in perspective of the entire Bible. It's that "not yet, but already" thing. Both are necessary to accomplish a task.

I am a detail person who easily gets overwhelmed. I can get overwhelmed just watching my fast and furiously working husband accomplish his own tasks in what seems like split second timing.

I wonder what tasks, what perspectives, what meanderings I need to reconsider by zooming in or zoning out.

I shall ponder…

Create

v.t., to produce through artistic or imaginative effort.

After a week's hiatus of cleaning… I was able to return to the piece I am working on for Yosemite Renaissance 2021. Its creation is a slow process. I am trying out and creating new techniques for granite and trees. (Yes, my new seam ripper and I have become great friends.)

When I returned to my now spotless, uncluttered, somewhat unfamiliar art room, I wondered if I could "create" in such an environment… I have claimed I couldn't, but turns out I can! Hmmmmmm.

My creative process doesn't seem connected to what's around me, but what's in front of me…the feel of the fabrics, their colors, their texture, the challenge of finding just the right colors needed from my "too many, but not enough" collection of fabrics and recycled men's ties.

As I look at this morning's sunrise… I wonder if it's possible to show its prespring character and color through fabrics… I suppose one day I will try, but for now…

I shall ponder…

Swooshing Drum

Swoosh: *v.*, the sound of air or water that is moving quickly.
Drum: *n.*, to make a succession of strokes, vibrations, or rhythmic beats.

I heard PO's heartbeat yesterday. That swooshing drum, pounding to a beautiful and healthy beat.

On another note, today, my gr-niece-lette, Lorelai, will be born. Though I can't hear it…within mama Tracy's tummy rests that same swooshing drum pounding to a similar, beautiful, and healthy beat.

It seems the great debate is not if the heart is, in fact, beating, but who has the "right" to determine its fate. Not my debate to contend with. Not a debate that will ever be agreed upon on this side of heaven.

Many moons ago…after prebirth testing, it was believed my daughter had a moderate possibility of spina bifida. More testing was required…pamphlets and counseling were offered on abortion. We traveled to a specialist who did what was "then" the highest technology 2D ultra sound and yes, had an amniocentesis done. (Do they even do those now days?)

I remember that moment the doctor found Elise's heartbeat… that same swooshing drum pounding to a similar, beautiful, and healthy beat. This time, however, we could actually "see" her heart beating for the first time! I looked at my husband and said, "I can't stop that heartbeat—whatever the cost." There was more "drama" in the pregnancy, but we walked with faith under God's omniscient, omnipotent, omnipresent sovereignty.

Now that healthy baby girl is having her own baby...what a beautiful song of worship to our Lord.

I shall ponder...

Good Morning, Swooshing Heartbeat of Lorelai Lei

This is truly your sunrise. Today you will surely be born. Your mommy and daddy will love you both uniquely and as vastly as your brother Charlie. They will render you love, care, prayer, protection, and guidance in the way that you should go. They will teach you about Jesus…who He is, that He created you, and desires for you to live with Him throughout eternity.

You have grandmas and grandpas that will love you as their own, but spoil you more. They will pray for you and gain unmeasurable joy watching you grow. They will always be there to support you and "hear" you.

You have aunties and uncles that will treasure you, take you on adventures, sleepovers where raw cookie dough will be consumed and teeth brushing is not required. They will offer you more cousin playmates and lifetime memories than you can imagine.

You have Great Grand's that will be amazed at family gatherings when they see your mommy or daddy's expressions mirrored on your face, and they will be ever so blessed.

You have so much beauty on this earth to explore…as large as a mountain, as small as a pebble and as soft as a feather.

Welcome Lorelai Lei.

Storm

~~~~~~

n., a disturbance of the atmosphere marked by wind, rain, snow, hail, sleet, or thunder and lightning.

My mind was everywhere but sitting in the presence of God this morning. I don't have a problem admitting it. It is nothing more than a truth. My truth.

I peeked out the window and saw a "storm a comin'" (in my head that thought was accompanied by a song from Music Man… something about a train). Anyway, my next thought was a sarcastic… yeah, a storm (figurative) probably is a comin'. I grabbed my iPhone and went outside to take the obligatory photo…

Once out there… I snapped a quick photo…sorta told the Lord I didn't have time to "chat" with Him this morning…again…nothing more than a truth, but I imagine the Lord lovingly snickered at me.

Out of the corner of my eye I saw a quick little chick-a-dee that momentarily captured my attention, which then caused me to see the presunrise photo from another perspective. It looked the same, but I saw it differently.

I love storms. Though this one I am viewing will likely not bring me any form of precipitation… I can imagine myself sitting in my chair later on in the day with an electric blanket keeping me warm, reading a novel, with a pot of soup on the stove. I mean…is there anything cozier?

The thing is, just because a storm is visible…doesn't mean it will necessarily "storm" on me. I just may find myself under the cozy wing of my Lord.

I shall ponder…

Sweet Song

Sweet: *adj.,* having the characteristic of a pleasant taste.
Song: *n.*, a poetic composition.

It takes only one tiny blackbird, on a light pole, singing a sweet song of worship to change the entire disposition of a stark, clean, sunrise.

It reminds me that it takes only one soft, gentle, pleasant, and sweet word to change the disposition of the one I am talking to, and likely myself as well.

I shall ponder…

Adventure

n., an exciting or remarkable experience.

Barry and I are partners for life. This year we will hit our thirty-fifth year. It hasn't been that hard to stick together through thick and thin...there has certainly been thick, and certainly thin, but it was just natural to stick together.

We love adventures...whether on foot or behind a wheel...we love to discover what is before us. Some of our best adventures have been by mistake...like when we made a wrong turn on a road in Kentucky...that green lawn, those white picket fences...beautiful horses, beautiful oak trees... Kentucky kindness.

Certainly, we can always find favorite adventures repeating the same trails, over and over in Yosemite.

Barry enjoys the great adventure of planning a road trip as much as the adventure of being on one. Though he pretty much does the planning of our adventures alone...it is not complete for him until I give my nod of approval.

Marriage is an adventure...there is always something before us...we may not always want to go the same direction, but it is just natural to stick together.

Adventures... I shall ponder...

Serenity

n., calmness of mind; tranquility of temper; placidity.

Right across from my prayer chair is a large (24"×36") piece of acrylic art created by my art mentor, TimMcMeansArt.com. I am keeping watch over him until he is purchased by his future owner.

He is a well-traveled raven with insightful eyes and weathered wings whose name is "Serenity."

He speaks to me. Not in a weird idol worship way, but he reflects so much wisdom within his serenity…

Hmmmmm… Maybe if I am wanting wisdom… I should first seek serenity…

I shall ponder…

Slow and Fast

Slow: *adj.,* moving or proceeding with little or less than usual speed or velocity.

Fast: *adj.,* moving or able to move, operate, function, or take effect quickly.

This morning I came out before the first peek of light began to show through the clouds…when it was completely black on the horizon. The sun rays began to peek through the horizon at what seemed both a slow and fast rate of time. In the overall sense…it seemed slow, but when I really began to focus on the intricate details…it was moving/changing fast.

So true about life. Life seems to move slow and fast at the same time.

At age sixty-three…my general focus on life is to slow down. I want adventure, but not too much adventure. I want excitement, but not too much excitement—the list goes on.

I want to plan, compartmentalize my life. But the truth is, it is changing every moment, and I ultimately have no control. I have the ability to plan for what I think "might" happen, the ability to react and respond to what does happen, and even "the choice" which of my attitudes to react and respond with, but I have no control; I don't like that. Just sayin'.

Yesterday, in my study, the Kings were provoking God to anger; in the very next chapter, Elijah appears and God shows him and the peeps he is with how to walk one step / one direction at a time. I believe God does that in my life, but that is the part where I want things to speed up. I don't want to take one step at a time in a specific direction. I want to know the entire picture, the whole enchilada (hmmm, Mexican for dinner?).

Anyway, "maybe" I don't have to worry about fast/slow, compartmentalizing or being out of control. I just need to make the most of the moment I am in.

I shall ponder….

We Will See

phrase, used in speech to say that someone will have to wait for the final answer.

I can't help it…after this last week… I have to recognize the reality of how fragile life is. What keeps spinning in my head is a phrase repeated to the husband of my daughter's BFF.

"We will see." Medical staff repeated this in response to questioning if his wife and twin babies were going to keep breathing after their birth. "We will see." I am unable to comprehend hearing those words.

I spent my entire sunrise time praying for them this morning. All are stable, but there are many steps yet to be taken for this young family with five under five. I had to ask the Lord to guide my prayers… I had no idea where to start…

Personally, I was challenged to focus on what is truly important in life. The grunt work of packing boxes is *not* important. Creating close ties with family is.

As I watch this sunrise, I am reminded of something I "know," not something "we will see," and that is…

"The Lord is my shepherd, I shall not want."

I shall ponder…

Wait

v.i., to remain stationary in readiness or expectation.

Certainly, the first word that came to mind for me this morning was "subtle." The sunrise was subtle, the fog was subtle, in the distance was the subtle sound of cows impatiently mooing for what I assumed was their morning hay. A few of the early riser Canadian geese were honking for their gaggle mates to awaken and fly to the golf course, an occasional caw of a crow overhead. Subtle…it was all subtle.

I was enjoying the sunrise, but was unhappy because I had neglected to charge both my iPhone and SLR. Soooo… I plugged my phone in and "waited."

Generally, my preference for photos is before the sun actually shines through.

In my "wait," the subtleness turned to greater beauty when I could peer at the fog with greater light. In perfect timing, my precious hubby brought me my iPhone that had "super charged."

Yes, there it is—the ponder—if I would just wait…wait when life is moving too fast before me…wait when life is not moving fast enough…wait on the Lord…

I shall ponder…

Moments

n., a comparatively brief, specific period of time.

I expected a dramatic sunrise this morning based on the wind patterns we have had. But it turned out to be a windy, yet soft sunrise. Unusual. I wanted to be disappointed, but I just couldn't.

My favorite parts of a sunrise are those few moments just before the sun appears…when all you see is a thin fiery line, just above the horizon. It starts where the sun will rise and works its way out. If you blink, you might miss it.

Moments… I have "moments." Moments when I literally have to stand still because of what I am experiencing. I often will say to Barry, "Hold on… I'm having a moment."

Sometimes, I have "secret moments" when dialoging with family. I do take moments to smell flowers, analyze their structure and beauty. Sometimes I have a "moment" when I am experiencing spasmistic (yes, my own word) back pain, and sometimes a "moment" because I am feeling no pain at all. I certainly have Holy Spirit-filled moments on my sunrise deck.

What if I lived every moment as a "moment"? So much to ponder here, soooo…

I shall ponder…

Stillness

n., the quality or state of being quiet, calm, silent.

I went down to the waterfront to view the sunrise with Barry this morning. It's so interesting how the movement of the boat, the cars, the water didn't seem to affect the "stillness" of the moment… they, in fact, pronounced it.

I have always been intrigued…challenged by passages in the Bible regarding "stillness." Certainly, Psalm 46:10, *"Be still and know that I am God."* But the one that tests my spirituality most is from Exodus 14:14, *"The Lord will fight for you, and you have only to be silent."*

Being silent before the Lord is not that hard for me when a small paddle boat is ruffling my waters, but when a barge comes through…it's much harder to be silent, to continue in stillness.

Anxiety vs. stillness.

Frustration vs. stillness.

Inner chatter vs. stillness.

The truth for me to ponder is; first, I must be "silent." Next I must be "still," *then*, I will "know" the one, true God who is fighting for me, fighting against anxiety, frustration, inner chatter—anything that keeps me from drawing near to Him, from glorifying Him…

I shall ponder…

—

Memories

n., the mental faculty of retaining and recalling past experience.

Right next to my coffee pot sits a Royal Dalton figurine of a little lady drinking tea. My mother-in-law (M-I-L) collected Royal Dalton and she wanted me to have her when she passed. Every morning when getting my coffee, this little lady reminds me of both my M-I-L and my F-I-L.

I have to admit... I never understood the collection of such expensive objects until my in-laws had passed and the object suddenly awakened sweet memories of them...especially of times we shared enjoying a good cup of tea. English style.

While the entire tea experience was soothing to my M-I-L and I, my F-I-L's need for efficiency would awaken a state of irritation from his normally gentle spirit. Without fail he would complain about the "string and tab" found on the tea bag, and its uselessness (It's useful to me...just sayin'). The tea must be nothing less than *hot*! The entire tea experience was shortened due to the calculated temperature check of each sip.

What am I doing consistently "with" my younger generations to create wonderful memories that will last a lifetime?

Could it be...sharing some of my nephew, JohnE's favorite tea over great and humorous conversation? Texting extended conversations at the Thanksgiving table (and hiding in the RV later on to finish them up) with my other nephew, Matt. Scouting the Brentwood farms for fresh fruit and veggies (buying and eating an entire loaf of the best sourdough bread ever that we are sure was laced with "something") with my niece, Brittany. Endless car adventures to share our "secret ponder places" with my other niece, Leanne. Definitely, a snuggle on the couch with a blanket and diet coke to watch endless episodes of Gilmore Girls with my daughter, Elise.

What I learned on our last road trip, and again here...is that these special times are created "with" each other. I hope they are as special to them as they are to me. I hope the pieces of art I have created for them will one day remind them of the special times we had together.

I shall ponder…

Truth

n., conformity to fact or actuality.

Before this sunrise, I was praying specifically in reference to "the belt of truth" and the armor of God. It is the first piece of armor scripture tells us to bustle on.

Truth. Truth connected to protection…it got me pondering… do I really seek truth when I am seeking protection?

I believe God is truth, and there is only one truth. So first I must seek God.

Truth cannot be separated from righteousness…righteousness is the perfect holiness of Christ…the polar opposite of sin. Next, I must seek righteousness.

Truth is the correctness, the sound wholeness of the Gospel… of all scriptural doctrine (Beyond the "Theology of Sandi.") Next, I must study scripture.

Truth is the sincerity of my character, intentions, words, actions. Frankly, the toughest one for me…it is not dependent on who Christ is, but who Christ is in me. *Yikes!* So probably not lastly, I must live in sincerity.

Again…do I seek "truth" when looking for protection?

I shall ponder…

Direction

n., the management or guidance of someone or something.

The darkened clouds were traveling north this morning. I captured a slow mo video of some geese flying west…while other geese were traveling east…clearly traveling in a direction…under the management of God.

I often feel I am wandering "aimlessly" while seeking direction from God. God clearly told the Israelites to "follow a cloud" while wandering in the desert, yet despite the clear direction…they grumbled, complained, and blamed Moses. Such a perfect example of me at times.

My cycle of direction can be, to ask God for direction, at some point direction is given. I respond to that direction; if it does not go as "I" would have liked to direct it, I grumble, complain, and likely find someone to blame. Ohhh to learn from history.

The thing is, what are my grumblings despite the clear direction of God? Certainly, I internally grumbled that our house has not sold in two weeks when I know the average time on the market is forty-five days. I am grumbling at the conflicting information being "spun" about COVID-19…when currently all I really need to do is not touch my face, wash my hands, and buy some more hand sanitizer.

I shall intend to seek God's cloud of direction and walk under it, walk step by step beneath it—maybe at times be called to stand still, but I shall intend to stay under it and ponder not…just stand in stillness.

For now, I will stand in stillness…

Later, I will ponder…

Name

n., a word or phrase that distinguishes a person or thing from another.

Though I am pretty sure PO will always stick as a beloved nickname, today I will know the name of my grandbaby.

This bridge is named after Helen Madere, a once-vice mayor of Rio Vista, but most call it the Rio Vista Bridge.

There are many names of God: Master, Shepherd, Provider to name a few, but my favorite is the simple yet powerful "Great I Am."

The first human was named "Adam," presumably from the Hebrew word for "ground," reminding Adam, and us, the first human was created from the ground's dust. Next was named Eve, a name that means "living" and distinguishes Eve's role as "the mother of all the living."

My name, Sandra, is Greek in origin and means "protector, defender of mankind" or "brave." Good call mom and dad! I think I am distinguished by the name "brave."

I have taken on names over the years…that I am working to "throw off" because they don't define who I truly am. Names I am not meant to distinguish myself with.

On the other hand, I have taken on names that do distinguish me…mama, auntie, SandiSays, and soon Grandma Saaan-Deeee! Certainly quirky, creative, and outspoken introvert define who I am.

What are the names you will distinguish yourself with sweet little PO due in July?

I shall pray and ponder…

n., freedom from restraint.

Liberty Jean will be the name of our new granddaughter. "Liberty" is a name Elise has loved for quite some time… Jean is a family name…my grandma, Jean…my mother-in-law, Norma Jean, and my sister-in-law, Nicki Jean.

My daughter shared this on an FB post: "We pray that Liberty has a relationship with Jesus so pure and genuine that those who are around her can't help but notice that this little girl has a joyous, wild and free spirit you can only have through liberation in Jesus Christ. We can't wait to meet you little kingdom shaker."

Liberty. Freedom. My husband and I fought hard for Elise to have the freedom in society to be who God made her to be…in fact, herself, a joyous, wild, and free spirit.

Our forefathers fought hard for American freedom.

Christ died for spiritual freedom.

The thing about American liberties and freedoms are…we seem to be constantly fighting for them and they need to come with boundaries of protection. The Bill of Rights was written as a safeguard for freedom of religion, speech, press, arms, and also protection of life, liberty, property, and in criminal and civil cases. American's have fought hard over the years to both expand and reduce the boundaries of both these liberties and freedoms.

The thing about spiritual freedom is, it is a freedom that can't be fought for by man. It was a one-time deal fought on the cross… the boundaries for spiritual freedom can't be changed and are simple and clear: *"Love the Lord your God with all your heart, with all your soul, with all your strength, and with all your mind, and love your neighbor as yourself"* (Mark 12:30).

"If you continue in My word, then you are truly disciples of Mine; and you will know the truth, and the truth will make you free" (John 8:31b–32).

I shall ponder…

Darkness

n., absence of light, clarity, or illumination.

I lost a friend, who is the son of my "bestie," to the darkness of mental illness this week. It is so confusing and dark, profoundly without any clarity. I am uncertain how to make sense of it all...how to help those who are left behind. I sought counsel.

Mental illness often "rears" itself in adolescence when hormones and puberty begin to change the body's chemistry. The youngster afflicted can't make sense of what they are feeling so do not know how to express it to others...the hiding begins. As they mature, their ability to hide also matures.

Mental illness is a disease. Like cancer...moments, hours of joy can fill the afflicted person, but the return to the reality of the disease can be plummeting.

Also, like in cancer, there are times when the ridden one decides "enough is enough" and determines to pursue freedom through death. Usually, the days following that decision are, in fact, the most joyous they have experienced since the onset of the disease.

In stillness, sadness, confusion, and my own sort of darkness, I shall ponder...

Light

n., the natural agent that stimulates sight and makes things visible.

It is hard to share about light when standing in the darkness with my friend.

This morning, while venturing out to retrieve my cup of coffee, I mistakenly turned the kitchen "overhead" lights on instead of the subtle ones underneath the cupboards. I was reminded how bright light in the darkness can hurt. But my eyes adjusted and I actually had a clearer view of the coffee I sloshed on the counter, and left to clean up later.

Scripture says: "*The light shines in the darkness, and the darkness has not overcome it*" (John 1:5).

Sometimes, light is merely evidence of our own darkness. Most times, for me anyway, it is something I can receive and hold on to within that darkness.

Darkness brings questions. Though light also brings questions, it can also provide answers. Answers offered by man can be a sloshy mess that needs to be cleaned up later. Answers offered by man can also present a pinhole of "light" that may hurt for a moment, but will adjust the eye and heart out of the darkness.

Even when in the midst of the deepest darkness I have ever experienced… I choose to believe that Jesus is the Light…that Light will set us free because the darkness cannot overcome it.

I shall ponder…

Ripples

v., to become lightly ruffled or covered with small waves.

I was quite drawn to the ripples in this morning's sunrise. Then I noticed them ever so small further back in the tiny section of sunrise as well. I couldn't really capture their true expression through my camera lens because a huge part of their beauty was movement.

Ripples. Besides ripples in clouds, there are beautiful ripples in water, ripples in potato chips, and of course, the "ripple down effect." I am unsure why the "ripple up effect" is not more considered and acted upon.

My husband always tries to intentionally smile at people he passes at the grocery store, McDonald's, etc. It is amazing the effect such a simple act can produce. A few of those strangers have later come back to tell Barry how that smile changed their day.

I have a friend who makes me homemade chicken soup whenever I am sick. It makes me feel loved, warm, and yes, it heals my soul. It has also inspired me to do the same.

What can I do today to start a ripple up effect?

I shall ponder…

Toilet Paper

n., a long strip of perforated paper wrapped around a paperboard core…often used for purposes other than originally intended, *i.e.,* blowing the nose, the draping of a human to create a wedding dress at a bridal shower…an interactive toy bringing great joy to a puppy dog.

The inner cardboard roll can also be used to create an unimaginable amount of necessary items such as a kaleidoscope, slinky, party poppers, seed starters, and more.

Why wouldn't the world be in an uproar at the inability to secure a two-year backup supply of an item in such "unprecedented" times as this?

I shall—sarcastically—ponder…

Presence

n., the area immediately surrounding a great personage, especially sovereign.

This morning while sitting in the fog, and the presence of God, I thought about, and was amazed at... God's many blessings upon my life. They have been abundant of late. But then, I remembered just several days ago...when I literally said, "Lord, I could use your blessing right about now."

As I sit here today, I now understand that the truest blessing, which is ever present...is to simply sit "in" His presence. When I am allowing myself to truly sit in His presence, I am aware of His many blessings on my life...large and small...complete provision and more.

However, when I am not allowing myself to sit in His presence... I am more aware of what I am missing...what I think I need...make that...what I want.

I don't have to be on my sunrise deck, in the stillness and silence to allow myself to sit in the presence of God. I must only acknowledge that He is there with me...always.

I shall ponder...

Friendship and Intimacy

Friendship: *n.,* a distinctively personal relationship that is grounded in a concern on the part of each friend for the welfare of the other, for the other's sake, and that involves some degree of intimacy.

Intimacy: *n.,* a close, familiar, and affectionate personal relationship with deep understanding.

Two of my closest friends dealt with unconnected tragedy this last week. What I have witnessed is, friendship, which holds that degree of intimacy...can be used to bring healing...when nothing else on earth seems to penetrate the wound.

Friendship can be delivering a meal with a hug and a wink of an eye that speaks volumes...with intimacy resonating.

Friendship can be simply sitting, cuddling in silence...with intimacy resonating.

Friendship can be receiving a phone call and prayer, while waiting in line at a crowded Safeway...with intimacy resonating.

Friendship can even be found in a sarcastic, politically incorrect comment, not to be shared in public, but only in the intimacy of friendship, which brings the first good laugh for the one in tragic grief.

Intimacy in friendships separates itself from acquaintances. Tragedy seems to surface that truth of intimacy, causing the cords of each to realign themselves.

Today... I shall pray for each of those women whose cords have aligned themselves with mine...causing me to be a stronger woman. I am thankful.

I shall ponder...

I shall pray...

I shall ponder...

Mentor

n., an experienced and noble adviser.

The pandemic quarantine offered Barry and I the chance to begin watching the *Star Wars* series. Believe it or not…until yesterday, I was a *Star Wars* virgin…untouched by its mastery and complexity.

I researched *Star Wars* "helps" online…knowing I would be lost without it. It was a good thing because almost immediately I was confused by the seemingly expendable "guys in white" who were not, in fact, "good guys."

A sense of excitement came as I actually connected imagery to that of rides in Disneyland, and even recognized spoken "Klingon." Maybe I was not a *Star Wars* virgin after all…hmmm.

The one thing that was clear to me…was that Obi-Wan Kenobi…was a mentor to Luke Skywalker. Without him…we'd all be lost in the ways of a Jedi and "The Force"…

I have an art mentor; he is, in fact, experienced, noble, and certainly an adviser. He has also offered to be my *Star Wars* mentor— what a guy!

The thing about my art mentor is, usually to my disdain…he does not tell me what needs to change to eliminate a "rough spot" in my art, but guides me to figure it out for myself. I suppose…that… is the "noble" part. He makes sure "my art" remains "mine" and not influenced by another.

Spiritual mentors are hard to find…we are all so broken. With certainty, I can study the Gospel, study the ways and words of Christ, which does not take me out of my "rough spots," but guides me through them.

The thing about the Lord is, He does not desire for me to be anyone other than who I was uniquely called to be. He has called me His workmanship…created in Him…to do good work, and I shall.

I shall also ponder…

Why

adv., for what purpose, reason, or cause; with what intention, justification, or motive.

I spent a long time on the deck this morning. If felt good. It had been weeks since I went out in the darkness and watched the ticktock changes in the sky as the sun began to rise over those Sierra Nevadas.

I prayed, I cried, I quietly sang a few songs, I watched the horizon, and I resisted getting close enough to God to ask...why. There are so many unanswered questions.

Unable to resist...my questions seemed to start simple, but then took me deeper and deeper into my soul.

Will my daughter be able to "share the love" at a baby shower? Will I be allowed to support my daughter and son-in-law during the birth of their baby? Will my son-in-law even be allowed in the room when his daughter is born? Very real questions that have been thrown out there.

All of those questions and many more are what I focused on so I could ignore the deeper questions of why. Why did a precious bright-eyed baby girl, given a miraculous and fresh, new start in life...die a simple death in her sleep. Why did one of the most selfless, caring, vibrant, and dry-humored, young men I know need to choose death to direct himself to peace? Why was a young wife, mother of a three-month-old, and strong woman of God unable to exit her vehicle following a fiery crash? Why?

Why...is clearly not mine to know. Which brings me to "who"—who does know? Clearly, the answer is God. Which brings me to "am I willing," willing to let my faith rest there? I cannot so clearly say, "yes." I will rest my faith there because, well, for one thing, they were not my children, but also, because my only other choice is to "not."

I shall ponder...if I can...

Inner Circle Friends

n., a small, exclusive, and intimate group of like-minded people sharing comradery and trust.

"ICFs," I don't make them easily. By choice.

This weekend allowed me time with several friends I don't get to spend enough time with. The thing is, it doesn't matter because our inner circle connectedness takes over and it is as if no time has passed. The "gnarly" (definition: extreme) thing is when you realize your ICFs daughter is now one of your very own ICFs! Crazy goodness!

The next generation...

I have learned so much, gained so much from their generation. It has been both blessed and easy to develop close friendships with my nieces and nephews. I have an especially close friendship with my daughter. Unfortunately, I have not figured out how to eliminate friction when my "mom meter" and "friendship meter" are both active. Currently, I am working on balancing between the two, but I will never turn my "mom meter" off completely.

When my daughter was preparing to marry her man, my "mom meter" was on full blast when she mentioned half the females in California were going to be her bridesmaids. Okay, it was only six, but my eyes were rolling. After a good ponder, I did come to realize the importance of her "peeps" standing with her on such a special day.

I began listing the names of ladies I consider my own ICFs. When I got to ten, I nearly had a heart attack; when I got to twelve, I determined I needed to drop two from the list. Yes, I am that crazy.

Why would I want to limit the amount of friendships in my inner circle? As I ponder… I have to wonder if it is a "control" thing. Upon further pondering it seems it is because I want to ensure I am able to be a very "present" friend whenever needed. I guess deep down that equals a "fear."

The Bible says that perfect love casts out all fear. I am not capable of perfect love on this side of heaven, but I can tap into the "One" who is.

How much friendship do I resist because of some sort of fear? Am I willing to tap into the One who casts out all fear?

I shall ponder…

Nothing

pn., not a single part of anything.

I prayed to receive God's "word" for me this morning. I got "nothing." Though God seemed silent…his silent presence again surrounded me in a way I do not feel in other times of my day.

Barry and I have been scouring stores in the early morning looking for hand sanitizer and masks for our son-in-law who is an "essential worker." We have come up with "nothing" except for a dear friend, my quilting cousin, our realtor, who is sharing the cleanliness of a pumper bottle with me.

Hours later…my sister-in-law sent me a link to a blog explaining how to sew a washable mask for nonhospital workers. Since this pondering gal is not shy on fabrics and even had the necessary interfacing and elastic on hand…a face mask prototype went into production.

We met our daughter and son-in-law for a social distancing, car to car lunch and I presented the prototype. He suggested a slight change to adjust for an earpiece he must keep in his ear. Face mask 2.0 is currently in production.

Sometimes…when you ask God for something, and it seems you get "nothing," there comes a point when you realize…something can still be made from it…

I shall ponder…

Mask

n., a cover or partial cover for the face used for disguise or protection.

Three days ago, in a galaxy far away (could I be watching to many *Star Wars* movies?), I had not even a hint of an idea that God would begin to use me in a "face mask" making ministry. It is a slow process with the cutting, pinning, sewing, marking, pinning, pleating, sewing (and seam ripping, here and there).

I prayed while making my son-in-law's masks yesterday. He is an "essential worker," coming across many people in a day, and going home to a pregnant wife...my daughter.

This morning when I awoke to many requests for masks, I was a bit overwhelmed. I soon realized, I didn't need to be... I just needed to focus on prayer for the mask's eventual and intended owner...not the mask itself.

I can say as a curvy, chunkster all my life... I learned at a very young age to put on a mask of humor to hide my insecurities. I carried that mask most of my life until as an adult I attended a community gym, where I learned I was strong and, most importantly, to "own" my curves. I shed that mask and to my delight...the humor remained.

What masks do I still put on in a day to "cover, disguise or protect" myself? How much strength am I expending to keep that mask on? Is it really worth it? What masks do I ridiculously put on before the Lord? Easily, the first thought that comes to mind is the mask of "I can do this!."

The thing I must ask myself about the mask of "I can do this!" is, is it in response to the Lord, properly put in place to shield me from worldly distraction? Or is it a mask of information I am telling the Lord which shields me from his commands and truth?

I shall take off my mask and...ponder...

Unexpected

adj., not regarded as likely to happen.

It was unexpected to awaken to the news yesterday that one of my daughter's bridesmaids brought her new baby girl into this crazy world at thirty-five weeks. Later on, it was unexpected news to find out that we had an offer on our house (since it is now a "misdemeanor" to show houses in our state). Even later still…it was unexpected to hear my (otherwise healthy) step-brother in Arkansas has tested positive for COVID-19.

Life is filled with "unexpected" moments…some change our lives for the moment…some change our lives forever.

My bestie who totally dislikes my beloved country western music sent me a video of her foot stompin', knee slappin' two-year-old granddaughter as she listened to a children's country music mix. It definitely changed my life for more than several moments, and likely, will change my bestie's forever!

The thing about unexpected moments is, it is fruitlessness to try and figure out why they happened. The fruit comes when we respond to the moment with love, joy, peace, patience, kindness, goodness, faithfulness, gentleness, and self-control…when we learn from those moments, and our lives are forever changed.

I shall ponder…

Coffee

n., a dark-brown powder with a strong flavor and smell that is made by crushing coffee beans.

I get great delight from my morning coffee…the taste, the caffeine, the smell, the warmth of the cup on my hands…quite the experience coming from a little brown bean.

I get even greater delight sharing a cup with my prayer partner on Tuesday mornings, because besides the taste, caffeine, smell, and warmth…comes prayer, laughter, tears, growth, and true fellowship.

Before we put our house up for sale, I had scripture written on a full-length mirror that was on the "inside" of our bedroom, bathroom door. The very first scripture I wrote on that mirror was "*For we are the aroma of Christ to God among those who are being saved and among those who are perishing*" (2 Cor. 2:15).

Obviously, I have pondered this verse often… It is actually a verse that has taken me a long time to unlayer. I started by just knowing, I wanted to be the sweet aroma of Christ.

What the Theology of Sandi unpacked was that I am not meant to be the aroma…the aroma is Christ, His righteousness, sacrifice and grace… I am merely the bean that beholds the aroma…a vessel that is used to speak forth, work forth, those heavenly spices, and yes, sometimes must be "crushed" in order for others to truly partake… even though some may smell the aroma, but never partake of the drink.

I shall continue to ponder…

Flying

adj., moving in the air.

I love the feeling of rushing wind in my face, through my hair. Before my back injury I gravitated easily to any activity that would provide such an occurrence, downhill skiing, parasailing, roller coasters, biking, and even long-distance running.

We saw a storm of snow geese yesterday on the Sacramento side of the Antioch Bridge. The wonder they produced. The freedom they have to fly...to enjoy the wind, yet their instinctual need to fly together in a sort of dancing wave to both migrate and find food.

I wondered if I were a goose...would I be that random "one" you come across...all by itself...hanging out? This shelter-in-place has revealed to me that I may not always want to socialize, but "migrating" with others is necessary...

Live streaming church...hanging out on the Marco Polo app with my Cali family... Face-timing with my Indiana family, and even chatting on the phone (one of my least favorite pass times) with my besties and sister-in-law have all become migratory acts of sorts.

There is a "safety" in numbers...especially when we are called to "fly" or "shelter" on the ground.

Scripture says: "*And let us consider how to stir up one another to love and good works, not neglecting to meet together, as is the habit of some, but encouraging one another, and all the more as you see the Day drawing near*" (Hebrews 10:24 and 25).

I shall ponder…

Essential

adj., necessary, vital, important.

It has always been clear to me that prayer is my "essential" ministry. I know that because I can't "not do it." I tried once…it didn't work. I don't make time for prayer…it grabs and holds my heart until it is done with me.

I said this before… I didn't see this face mask making ministry coming. Though it likely is not another one of my essential ministries…it certainly is an essential ministry. I am honored to be called to task…despite one broken machine and bandages on my finger tips from those nasty pins rebelling against multiple layers of fabrics.

I see others being called up, establishing FaceTime groups to encourage and daily devotional videos (meant for student ministry, but I rebelliously am watching them anyway!) and a woman from my Santa Clara Valley family's church who gave her name and number to an anxious, vulnerable, elderly couple standing in line at a grocery store, so she can begin to shop for them, just to name a few.

Also "essential" are the ministries being done at home. Conversations and prayer that would likely have never had time to happen…living rooms turned into cardboard runways, complete with card board parking garages and a church…storm doors in Indiana turned to a child's hand painted stained glass…almost daily FTs with shut-in great-grandmas…walks for newlyweds and restless children.

I almost didn't go out on the deck this morning; it looked so gray and uninviting, and I was cozy and warm inside, but I did, and what I realized is…

At first glance, something may seem gray and uninviting, but when you make yourself available, and eventually immerse yourself within it…you begin to hear a word, a personal call, maybe an essential ministry becomes clear.

It was certainly gray and uninviting for Christ on that cross, but it was essential.

I shall ponder…

Livestream

n., a broadcast of a live event streamed over the internet.

Many of us will be livestreaming our church service this morning. I could listen to the audio feed available anytime, for my convenience, but there is a certain joy in receiving it real-time with my other church family.

I can't deny…part of the joy of this livestreaming is knowing that my pastor likely, previously, secretly…made an agreement with himself not to ever do such a thing…except in obedience to God… assuming God would never ask him to plow forward into such a world (really…our church didn't even have audio feed until several weeks ago), and here we are. Surprise!

It's not that he is against livestreaming…it's that he doesn't want temptation to be anything other than himself as he delivers The Word of God. A humble, honest, spiritually academic man whose favorite saying used to be "It's a good thing we're not livestreaming!"

The Theology of Sandi wonders…in all the "omni's" of God (omnipotence, omnipresence, omniscience) is God livestreaming, of sorts, us…or…are we, Him? Clearly, the omni's of God are always livestreaming us (no technology needed), but we must behold an actual piece of those omni's, the Holy Spirit, a technology of sorts, to livestream Him.

The thing is, livestreaming can be something that is on in the background as we go get our cereal…have a conversation about what we should "take out" for dinner, or it can be our focus…even if we are in our jammies.

"For all who are led by the Spirit of God are sons of God" (Rom. 8:14).

We are not led to do "nothing," but in fact, "something." It may be to gather with our church family via livestream to "focus" for an hour. It may be to "connect and encourage" one with a phone call; it may be to focus our head to the carpet to intercede for medical staff, essential workers, our leaders, and those afflicted by the virus.

I shall ponder…

Already but Not Yet

theological concept, that believers are actively taking part in the kingdom of God, although the kingdom will not reach its full expression
until sometime in the future.

This "theological concept" kept coming to mind this morning…

In this morning's photo, the sun had already "risen," but not yet
shown through the clouds.

According to the Theology of Sandi…some are already chosen,
but have not yet been adopted…some are already adopted, but not
yet feasting at the table…all who believe, are already experiencing the
grace and mercy of our Lord, but not yet experiencing His full glory.
I believe we are wired to yearn for the next step toward experiencing
God's full Glory.

The thing is, we bring that "wiring" into our personal lives.
We already have plenty of clothes, but we yearn for trendier ones…
we already have a car, but we yearn for a better one. In other words,
we already have stuff, but we are constantly yearning for more. For
me, it is shoes, a truck, and fabric… I have finally met my quota in
sewing machines!

We must accept this "wiring" for what it is, a point of tension.
On the other side of heaven…it won't be, but until then, it is. The
wiring was designed to yearn us toward God's complete glory—not
a new truck, fabric, or the pair of cute tennis shoes in transit right
now…to my home.

I am not saying the purchase of those items are wrong... I am just challenged to consider the source of my yearning. What is it drawing me toward...

Dang-nab-it... I shall ponder...

Sandwich

n., a food consisting of meat, cheese, or spread, layered between two pieces of bread.

We took a trip across the Delta to make some mask deliveries and do some grocery shopping. As it neared lunch time and our second Safeway in search of flour, I texted Barry in the store and begged him to buy me a ham and cheese sandwich layered with their luscious olive loaf and aioli spread. I had been hankerin' for a good healthy sandwich for days!

Barry soon returned with a few groceries, my sandwich, and no flour. It was determined Barry would stop at McDonald's after our next mask delivery to get he and my mom some lunch as well. I couldn't help myself… I peeled the wrapper off of that ole' sammy the second it touched my hands. No waiting, no manners, and no regret!

I was so enamored by this sandwich, I shared on our family Marco Polo app. A discussion of our favorite sandwiches, spreads and aioli ensued. We all had visions of sandwiches dancing in our heads.

The thing about a sandwich is, the layers are "generally" evenly spread across the bread. (Taco Bell…no one wants a bite of pure sour cream at the end of their burrito!).

> *For this very reason, make every effort to supplement your faith with virtue, and virtue with knowledge, and knowledge with self-control, and self-control with steadfastness, and steadfastness with godliness, and godliness with brotherly affection, and brotherly affection with love. For if these qualities are yours and are increasing, they keep you from being ineffective or unfruitful in the knowledge of our Lord Jesus Christ.* (2 Pet. 1:5–8)

What am I layering between the safety of God's wings? Is it virtue, knowledge, self-control, steadfastness, godliness, brotherly affection, and love? Am I layering these virtues evenly across my day, or is it a firehose or trickle showing blasted at the end of my burrito? Am I sharing these virtues with enthusiasm to others, causing a hunger for more layers? Are these layers fruitful and effective in my life?

I shall ponder…

Refuge

n., protection or shelter from danger or hardship.

Today we took a "field" trip across the street to check out the pond-o-minium where the Canadian Geese gather at night. There were hundreds of mallard ducks and a gregarious group of pelicans hanging out there. The pond is usually pretty quiet during the day, so we were not sure what the "gig" was.

I enjoyed the fresh air and crackle of dry sticks and grass as I began to venture out to get a closer look at the birds. I was pretty much living my own scene from Duck Dynasty. I saw many "snake holes" on my expedition, so sought "refuge" in a raised, cement slab not too far from the car…we all know that snakes don't cross cement lines…right?

It is so peculiar how I felt "safer" on that raised, cement slab. The problem was… I eventually had to leave that slab to return to greater safety in our car. I was not a fan. I had moved from Duck Dynasty to Survivor Amazon…enjoy the show…not the journey, but refuge was soon found within the "quarantine" of our vehicle.

After pondering… I realized that cement slab offered me visual clarity against immediate danger. Spiritually speaking…we need that clarity and protection because we live in a fallen world and "snakes are everywhere."

The Lord offers us that visual clarity against temptation, but sometimes… He calls us to skip across a land, snaked with danger… to get us to greater protection "on the other side." God has provided us armor against such attacks (Ephesians 6), but ultimately, the protection we seek is eternity with Christ.

God does not promise that earthly harm will not come to us, but he does promise that *nothing* can separate us from His love… from Himself, which is where true security can be found.

"When we seek refuge in the Lord we are hard pressed, but not crushed; perplexed but not in despair; persecuted, but not abandoned; struck down, but not destroyed" (2 Cor. 4).

I shall ponder…

Ten

n., a set or group with ten elements.

My daughter and I had a well-needed social distanced, "curbside pickup" lunch at her (now, "my") favorite Thai restaurant... Rice Barn Thai Eatery. *Amazing* food...*great* people!

Barry and I have been trying to bless our favorite restaurants with orders and healthy tips. I had a tightly folded, almost forgotten $10 bill hiding in the back of my phone. I grabbed the bill and offered them a 50 percent tip. They humbly and ever so thankfully accepted.

We also have disciplined ourselves to offer our tithe (a tenth) to our church...as usual. We all *must* continue to financially support our church homes during this pandemic. Find that "give" button on your church website before livestreaming. Write that check.

In scripture, we have the Ten Commandments which God gave man to live in peace and unity. They are man's responsibility to God.

We have the ten plagues. They are both an act of judgment on Egypt and the fulfillment of a promise to Abraham...that God would set His people free.

And of course, we have our ten fingers and toes that allow us the "action" to offer a tip blessing...to tithe to our church...to maneuver in ways that bring unity and peace, and walk us to freedom through that Red Sea.

I shall ponder...

Consider

~~~~~~

v. tr., to think about carefully, especially before making a decision.

I am having a hard time keeping track of "mask" orders because they are coming in from text, email, several groups on FB and *waaayyy* too many feeds within those groups. Even the postal workers who have helped Barry mail orders off are requesting them.

I had this brilliant idea to use an Etsy account to funnel orders through. *Genius*, but *not*.

I set up my shop. There was so much to consider: photos, product description, price point (I have felt this was a ministry God called me to, for my community, so set a price at $1 per mask), features that allow for quantities available and shipment options.

I headed over to FB to write a post with my Etsy shop ready to organize requests. As I was writing "said" post… I kept getting email notifications…it became annoying and I thought maybe I was getting "hacked" so went to investigate.

To my bewilderment…my shop had "sold out" on masks. I had orders coming in from all over America. What I failed to "consider" was that while FB can be "private." Etsy is not.

Again, my life becomes portrayed right out of a sit-com episode from Big Bang Theory. Penny Blossoms are in production!

No time to ponder…

Ministry

n., the act of serving.

The days following the resurrection of Jesus were filled with over five hundred additional sightings of Jesus, and the realization, especially for the disciples…that ministry begins.

Ministry begins in the home…to our spouses, our children, our parents, our siblings. It branches out to our church, our friends, our community, our state, our country, our world. The key is not to get lost within the needs of people, but to get lost within our service to the Lord. To keep our focus on glorifying him…right where we are at.

Easier said, than done. Sometimes when I focus too heartily on ministering to people, I lose my ability to let the Lord minister to me, to prepare me, teach me, grow me, love me.

Sometimes, when I focus too heartily on ministering to people I lose my ability to remember I am "really" ministering to the Lord. In steps frustration and weariness. I want to be used to show off "my" strength…instead of "His" strength…forgetting true spiritual power is made perfect in weakness.

Sometimes, when I focus too heartily on ministering to people, I use my ability to grope for my own destiny…instead of allowing The Lord's destiny to come to me. I want to tell my own story instead of allowing God's story to be worked out in me.

Sometimes, when I focus too heartily on ministering to people I forget to walk humbly, fruitfully, and cheerfully with Christ…right where I am at.

Sometimes, I don't focus on ministry at all, and as long as I am keeping my focus on the Lord and obedience to the nudging of the Holy Spirit… I suspect I am right where I am supposed to be…

I shall ponder…

Protection

n., a cover or shield from exposure, injury, damage, or destruction.

This morning I danced to the kitchen because my favorite creamer was back in stock and now in my fridge. I shook that plastic container and unscrewed the top to find that ever so tightly vacuum sealed aluminum shield. Excitement diverted. I could just pop it with some scissors, but am compelled to remove it cleanly with my fingers. Not an easy task!

As I was struggling to unseal the vacuum...my diverted excitement was immediately transformed to appreciation. I now clearly saw this seal for what it was...protection. I can take "protection" a bit for granted. This new world we are living in has changed that, and that's a good thing.

The Father has commissioned himself to provide, protect and care for me. His protection is sustaining...over battles I see and many more I do not see. The challenge is for me to receive it...appreciate it...honor it...even when that protection is different from what I like or expect.

The term "hedge of protection" is often used in prayer. I have not come across the actual term in scripture but have come across a hedge of blessing God offered Job. The blessing included protection, but was also lifted to see who Job really trusted and loved.

The thing about a hedge is, instead of standing back to worship and be thankful to my Lord...my curiosity draws me near to peek at and listen to the train wreck of rumors on the other side. I hear the lies of the enemy, but I continue to listen anyway. The battle for my soul is won, but I reveal a tiny piece of my vulnerability through that hedge anyway.

I am a very curious person...very academic...that is a good thing when used for the glory of the Lord. But I must be intentional to use it to His glory, and not against it...those times that I try to peek through a key hole of doors that have been closed because I long for what I believe is on the other side...those times when I draw near to what I know is gossip, especially when it is about me…those times I listen to the lies that I am anything less than made in the image of God.

The thing is, protection is not in the hedge…it is in the Lord. Yes, in blessed protection… I shall ponder…

Armor

~~~~~~~~~~~~~~~~~~~~~~~~~~~~~~~~~~~~~

n., a defensive covering, worn to protect the body against weapons.

I saw my daughter, outside of a car, from afar, yesterday. I was so taken aback by how little Liberty has taken over a larger form in her mommy's tummy.

I would be remiss if I didn't admit that I have had concern for my pregnant daughter through this pandemic. She and her husband, an essential worker, have quite the system in place for when he comes home each night. I have my own system in place for the three of them each morning...it is called prayer.

I do pray for my heart's desire for them, health, a full-term delivery, that COVID restrictions will allow them to hold and bond with their newborn following birth...protection from viruses in general, and more...

I am made aware in my prayers that we are most protected by what we can't see, the armor of God, then what we can see, a mask, and sanitizer.

The armor of God consists of truth, righteousness, peace, faith, salvation, and the Holy Spirit. These are the things a true warrior prays for, and yes, they come in maternity size!

Though I am free to pray for my heart's desire...where true protection lies is in praying for the armor.

I shall ponder...

The Belt of Truth

Belt: *n.*, a flexible band worn around the waist or over a shoulder to hold up clothing, secure tools, or weapons.

Truth: *n.*, conformity to fact or actuality.

I hate belts...that's my truth...just sayin'.

Belts do serve a purpose though...they hold everything in place. We are instructed to put on the whole armor of God...not just pieces.

The word "belt" in Ephesians 6:14 translates to a "girdle," shall we say the "level 3 sculpting Spanx" of God? Again, not comfortable. However, those GodSpanx keep all the parts of the armor in place while still allowing them movement. It preserves firmness in the midst of COVID-19 bread and snack baking.

It is "truth" that gives consistency and firmness to our conduct. It is a kind of perfection offered in grace...sincerity of character; sound and correct doctrine and an uprightness of life. Well, that would be found in the Gospel story.

I need these GodSpanx of truth because I am guided sometimes by principle, and sometimes by interest. I have doubts, difficulties, hopes, and fears, that divert my alertness...excess that wants to create that muffin puff outside of the girdle.

However, when the GodSpanx remain firmly, constantly in place...it is a means of keeping me close to God...it is the state of my heart answering to God's truth; the inward, practical acknowledgment of the truth of who I am without that girdle on and the outward truth of who I am with it on...a truth that strengthens me against the assaults and attacks of the Evil One.

I shall ponder...

Breastplate of Righteousness

Breastplate: *n.*, a plate worn over the torso to protect from injury.
Righteousness: *n.*, purity of heart and rectitude of life; conformity of heart and life to the divine law.

The breastplate of righteousness guards our hearts and lungs… our spiritual vitals. We can "check our vitals," but only Christ can do the work to save our lives, which he did through the cross and resurrection. Loosely thought, the righteousness of the resurrected Christ are those paddles that bring us from spiritual death to life.

The thing about the breastplate of righteousness is, while we must hunger, thirst, and seek it, we can't do anything to earn it; we can only receive it, a gift issued for eternity at that first moment of repentance to Christ. We then have the responsibility to care for and use that armor daily…otherwise, our most vulnerable self is open to the piercings, lies and direct attacks of Satan to our hearts and lungs.

I suppose the question is how do we "put on" that armor? I conclude: repentance, sincerity of heart, and by avoiding what may "ensnare" us when we do find ourselves facing temptation.

I shall ponder…

Shoes

n., an outer covering of protection for the human foot typically having a thick or stiff sole.

While I hate belts, I do love shoes. Over the years, my appreciation for the "perfect" shoe has shifted. The perfect shoe could be calculated by cuteness and ability to match my work outfit. (I once owned a pair of Jimmy Choo shoes, which our dog, in fact, "chewed.") I now calculate shoe perfection based on comfort and support…aka, UGGs, Crocks, and Birkenstocks!

If I were to create the perfect shoe of readiness…it would be a morphism of a sturdy hiking boot to travel me easily over piercing rocks and mud, a lightweight running shoe, an ultrasupportive, and quick-to-put-on Birkenstock, the warmth and comfiness of UGGs, and yes, I suppose I could add that offensive Jimmy Choo "point" with recognizable colors.

Paul tells us in the Ephesians 6 armor scriptures to "stand," "withstand," and "stand firm," to be "ready" in both perseverance and the power of God to go wherever Christ would lead us for his sake…to do and suffer as he wills…to not fall and accept the terms of his "peace" when warfare comes, which would be faith in Christ.

The shoes are not the Gospel itself, but the "readiness.," given by the Gospel, to go with a heart settled, resolved and prepared. To publish the gospel of peace through my own story…that moment by moment thing that happens when detours, warfare and even the possibly complacent feelings of restful peace come.

God's peace is the sure, firm, supportive, protective, and comfy foundation of Christ on which I stand. A foundation that gives me readiness from the Gospel, to share the Gospel, which is peace. Readiness and peace are so intertwined they are hard to unlace… then again…why would I want to?

I shall ponder…

Side note: I realized my shoes rest directly next to the chair I use to go to my knees on…the warrior, prayer section of my closet… now when that earthy smell hits my nose while in prayer… I will remember…to be ready.

Shield of Faith

Shield: *n.*, a broad piece of armor, varying widely in form and size, carried apart from the body, as a defense against swords, lances, arrows, etc.

Faith: *n., "Now faith is the assurance of things hoped for, the conviction of things not seen" (Heb. 11:1).*

While the breastplate of righteousness is a shield to our spiritual heart and lungs…the shield of faith is a movable piece of protection over a soldier's entire armor covering the Christian's character and protecting against flaming darts.

These flaming darts come at that moment of disappointment, regret, anger, fear, loneliness, suspicion, doubt, temptation, annoyance. To be protected against them, I must "move" my shield of faith from one fiery dart to another. Yes, war is exhausting…

Though identification and knowledge of the dart, or its shooter…can help me maneuver my shield…it is faith, a belief in the truth of God, trusting his promises, that extinguishes those flaming darts…

So the question comes, do I spend more time maneuvering my shield, believing in God's promises, or more time analyzing the dart and its shooter?

I can tell you it has been a personal struggle for me lately. My faith is not shaken, but I am weary from maneuvering that shield against fiery darts; it just seems easier to take a break and get pierced a time or two or ten….

The problem is, those piercings create sores, scabs, and scars I become infatuated with, and pick at.

I am beginning to understand the importance of focusing on the shield, the faith, and determine to not divert my focus to scars, scabs, and fiery darts.

As I pull my focus back to the promises of God, I realize I can do it by rote, so why don't I hold it up in the first place? I suppose because I spend my time putting my pity pants on instead of lacing the shield with God's promises.

"For I know the plans I have for you, declares the Lord, plans for welfare and not for evil, to give you a future and a hope. Then you will call upon me and come and pray to me, and I will hear you. You will seek me and find me, when you seek me with all your heart" (Jer. 29:11–13).

I shall ponder…with all my heart…

The Helmet of Salvation

Helmet: *n.,* a form of protective gear worn to protect the head, skull, human brain.

Salvation: *n.,* deliverance from the power and effects of sin.

I cherish the photos I receive of my great nieces and nephews riding their preferred mode of "wheels," with helmets that seem larger than their entire body. That helmet seems to offer great confidence for both child and parent to "feel the wind," or at least the wings of a drive-by insect. A child dare not go to combat on the open road without it on. So is true with a battle helmet…especially a spiritual battle helmet…a soldier dare not fight without it on.

The helmet of salvation must both be issued by God for his own purpose and taken by man as a gift to play out and protect man in that purpose. God wills to save; we are safe and confident when we take the salvation which He gives.

When a soldier suits up for battle, or a child for the open road… the helmet is the last piece of armor to go on. The final act of readiness in preparation for fearless combat. It protects the brain, the command station for the rest of the body.

The helmet of salvation is issued at the point of salvation. When a child receives the gift of a bicycle, a helmet is also given. The child may sit on the bike in the living room where the gift was given, but it is when he heads out to the combat field of rocky landmines, uneven pavement, and the "incoming" that the eternal perspective of the helmet begins to take hold.

As a "saved by grace" Christian, I must intend and continue to study and learn the Bible and all that my salvation includes inside and out.

I shall ponder…

The Sword of the Spirit

Sword: *n.*, a weapon with a long blade for cutting or thrusting that is often used as a symbol of honor or authority.

Holy Spirit: *n.*, the third Person of the Trinity through whom God acts, reveals His will, empowers individuals, and discloses His personal presence in the Old and New Testament.

The sword is the only piece of offensive weaponry mentioned in the Ephesians 6 passage.

In my days of working for a military defense contractor, I learned that an offensive weapon hits a direct target, where a defensive weapon is a general shield against attack and keeps the enemy from getting too close. The sword of the Spirit is both.

Paul defines the sword of the Spirit as the "Word of God," which is living, powerful, sharp, piercing, and discerning. God's truth and promises are not meant to just cut the flesh, but pierce all the way to the innermost soul.

The sword belongs to the Holy Spirit, and is issued to us for battle. It is best represented by trained soldiers. Jesus, our example, demonstrated how valuable it is to be grounded in the Word of God when he accurately prophesied Scripture to deflect Satan's attacks of temptation in the desert. It is the undisciplined apprentice that quotes scripture out of context.

To properly wield the sword of the spirit, I must study the Bible carefully, understand how it all fits together—chapter, book, and the Bible as a whole, I must keep my sword sharp, allowing me to precisely slice between good and evil.

Paul lists only one weapon because I only need one weapon. There is no enemy the Word of God, coupled with His Spirit, cannot defeat. And so, armed only with my sword, I step out to fight my enemies head-on. The struggle is immediate. The struggle is real. The struggle is in front of me, and so is the sword.

I shall ponder...

Perspective

n., the capacity to view things in their true relations or relative importance.

Months ago, I watched as a large group of cows traveled to a new pasture via the Airport Road behind our house. Yesterday, it was sheep. I'm gonna miss this place!

This morning it was cows again. Barry and I heard cows loudly protesting as a black and white pup barked them into correct position. We ran out to the deck to watch (admittedly, more excited to watch the dog do his thing than watching the cows). As we peered over the fence...we saw nothing. The noise was coming from the other side of the airport, and it was just quiet and calm enough for the noise to travel.

Having the "capacity" for perspective is an art, or is it? Maybe it is that armor I have been pondering on...all wrapped up in prayer.

My spiritual battles do involve darkness and the spiritual forces of evil, but honestly, sometimes they just involve myself. You know that thing...we are our own worst enemy.

It seems the armor has a lot to do with perspective...righteousness, peace, faith, salvation, the Holy Spirit Word of God, and those GodSpanx that hold everything, including our perspective, in check.

Prayer does not actually seem to be a piece of the armor. Quite a ponder here...

The thing about armor is, it is meant for battle.

The thing about prayer is, it is meant for always *"praying at all times in the Spirit, with all prayer and supplication. To that end, keep alert with all perseverance, making supplication for all the saints"* (Eph. 6:18).

I shall ponder...

Determination

n., firmness of purpose; resoluteness.

While watching sheep be herded to another location the other morning, I couldn't help but notice a few sheep determined, and I mean "determined," to go the opposite direction of the parade route. It wasn't until they "heard" the whistle of their "herder," that they finally succumbed to their destiny.

The thing is, those several "determined" sheep did not know the greatness of the pastures that lay ahead…directed by a shepherd more determined to protect and care for them than they could for themselves…

This morning I watched another form of a herd, a gaggle of hundreds of Canadian Geese, flying to their new northern destination. No gaggle-herder, tractor, or cute black-and-white dog in tow, but certainly a lot of communication was going on.

I am intrigued by the contrast of the two, but I am more intrigued by their similarities…"determination."

Most of the sheep were "resolved," obedient to their destination, but those few that were not…were determined for the pastures of old.

The geese on the other hand, put all of their determination in moving toward their northern goal…communicating, shifting positions…while still staying in a placement that benefits all, and is rather beautiful to watch.

I must ponder…

What are my determined destinations? Am I swooning for pastures of old? Am I obediently being herded toward a new destination while determined to communicate disapproval to the shepherd? Are my destinations God directed…often causing constant communication and shifting of positions that benefits all…rather than "self"? Is my movement glorifying and beautiful to watch?

Yes, I shall ponder…

Hairspray

n., a solution sprayed on to a person's hair to keep it in place.

Yesterday my mom and I enjoyed watching the movie *Hairspray*.

Hair has natural movement. So do I. I like to walk, hike, exercise, and dance, but my greatest moments of desired movement seem to come when God asks me to wait. So what's up with that I ask!?

Wouldn't it be great if there was a Holy Spirit "solution" that could be sprayed on our minds and actions when the Lord calls us to wait?

The thing about hair spray is, it doesn't last for an extended time…it requires continual reapplication…until the hair no longer has resemblance of movement found within natural hair.

I think sometimes I try to apply a "solution," of sorts, to my will. It is not hard for my will to be in constant movement, but not so much when I am called to wait. It is a reasonable tool for success at first. But if I don't get the desired results, I just keep spraying it on…over and over…until my focus shifts from keeping my will in place to frustration with the "solution" that is not giving me those desired results.

So what is the "solution?"

Well, I suppose the solution is not in a solution, but in the wait…in stillness. It is so much easier to apply a solution that requires movement than waiting in stillness.

"*The Lord is good to those who wait for him, to the soul who seeks him*" (Lam. 3:25).

I shall ponder…

Bamboozled

~~~~~~~~~~~~~~~~~~~~~~~~~~~~

v., thrown into a state of confusion or bewilderment.

My favorite example of bamboozled comes from an absolute favorite *Friends* episode. In the words of Joey, "You spin the Wheel of Mayhem to go up the Ladder of Chance. You go past the Mud Hut, through the Rainbow Ring to get to the Golden Monkey, you yank his tail, and *boom*, you're in Paradise Pond!"

There are other rules such as holding your breath while questions are being read and bonuses such as "the hopping bonus" which can only be used during the super speedy round. There is a "backward bonus," which requires an answer be repeated backward.

This pandemic, quarantined, social distancing, virus thing has made me ponder the complexities I have bamboozled my life into being. I have let our country's best strategies bamboozle me away from Paradise Pond where lies my family, my church, and my besties.

I am rethinking the "essentials" in my life.

While Zoom did its best for our family Easter dinner, there is a beauty in sitting together around the same table, partaking of the same food, sharing, discussing, and debating with the music of more than one voice being heard at a time.

While I enjoyed "virtual church" at first, I now miss praising the Lord in song with other worshippers. I crave the reverence and lack of distraction our church holds during our pastor's sermons. I truly miss the smiles, encouragement, hugs, and love I receive from my church family.

My bestie needs me in this time…while my steady, calm voice and occasional belly laugh over the telephone sustains her, it is touch and hugs she is truly needing.

My prayer partner and I will both be moving in separate directions soon… I have not done well in meeting up with her weekly by phone… I realize I must make correction, because that time and relationship is "essential."

How many times have I been bamboozled with silly "rules" and proposed "bonuses" that take me away from the true essentials that will direct me to Paradise Pond?

I shall ponder…

Blessings

~~~~~~

n., something promoting or contributing to happiness, well-being, or prosperity.

Yesterday, I received quite the blessing when my geese friends flew directly in my line of focus as I was about to take a photo. Timing was everything. The timing of the geese, with the timing of the sunrise, with the timing of my camera that was focused and prepared for a shot, against a quite remarkable sunrise. That *was* a blessing! Or was it?

This morning I searched scripture related to "blessing." My non-concise study (thus, Theology of Sandi), revealed that Old Testament blessing seemed to be focused on promise or special favor by God which resulted in joy and prosperity, and had a counterpart of curse which brought earthly drought, disease, and depravation.

The New Testament blessing does not seem to be focused on material, but on spiritual and is generally used to designate that one "is" favored by God. There is a counterpart of pain, difficulty, and suffering, but that counterpart is part of the blessing…not the curse, because it brings us closer to God.

The conundrum here is that I find myself desiring Old Testament prosperity and material blessing while living in the redeemed world of New Testament spiritual blessing.

What material blessings am I hungering for that brings a counterpart of spiritual drought, disease, and depravation? Are my deep-seated needs fueling comfort or a blessing toward a deeper desire for God? Am I allowing my trials to be a channel for the eternal blessing of sanctification (to make holy) or the earthly temporal blessing?

Hmmmmm…

Yes, I shall ponder…

Lines

n., a one-dimensional figure, which has length but no width. It is made of a set of points which is extended in opposite directions to infinity and is determined by two points in a two-dimensional plane.

In nonmathematical terms, a line is the same definition…with 100 percent gray area.

Lines are often used to separate things…right from wrong, states on a map, the direction cars are to travel on a road, and in this morning's sunrise it separated the clouds from clarity.

Yesterday, my daughter and son-in-law had to make some tough decisions about time following the birth of little Liberty Jean. Medical professionals have concern for another surge of COVID-19 once our state begins to "open up." Authoritative lines are being drawn…no emotion involved, just clarity.

Yesterday, I spent the morning chatting with my nephew, planning a surprise for my mom's birthday. My entire east/midwest family was to travel out west to create more memories for my mom during the time of LJ's birth. I researched Airbnbs and planned day trips. I was in "emotion, no clarity" mode when I learned of the hard lines our health provider will keep in place for birthing parents and newborns…especially if they come in contact with "those who have traveled."

This morning I pondered on yesterday's happenings, and "lines." I realized the best line to focus on is actually the plumb line. It dangles freely, back and forth, until it finds "exact vertical," defining a straight path and foundation for the precious cornerstone. It is not changed by the whims and sway of the one who holds the line. It remains true.

I shall ponder…

Emotions

n., a natural instinctive state of mind deriving from one's circumstances, mood, or relationships with others.

I've had a lot of overbearing emotions the last few days...the "why" of that is an entirely different ponder. What I pondered on my deck this morning was understanding emotion itself, and most importantly, what the Bible says about them.

Emotions are involuntary. To repress them is to repress myself. I don't like to repress myself, just sayin'. (I know a few of you are chuckling out there!)

On the other hand, reality and the command to love dictates if the "expression" of my emotion is rational or irrational, just or unjust, appropriate or inappropriate.

I suppose God designed my emotions to be a benchmark that reports information to me...showing me where my hope really lies... not a dictator that controls or manipulates me...quite the dichotomy.

In scripture, God tells us about fear, delight, anger, anxiety. He tells us to exult, rejoice, hope, be glad and thankful...there's more. God commands this obedience "from the heart," not the head, because when motivation comes from my head, all I am left with is moralism.

The thing is, "emotions are a wonderful gift to color life, but they make terrible gods" (written in my Bible, I don't know who said it first). They are wired into my fallen nature giving both sin and Satan access to manipulate me away from faith.

What emotions am I displaying without repression that bring wonderful color to life? What emotions are dictating me away from faith...away from God? Am I expressing my emotions in a way that realizes that the glory of God is at stake?

Quite the ponder...

Toast

n., sliced bread browned on both sides to make hot, brown, or crisp.

Best served with smushed avocado, dried cranberries, and lightly roasted pine nuts…just sayin'.

My mom is making toast right now. The smell is oozing its way through the kitchen window. I barely noticed the smell each morning while on the deck, but since I began working on losing forty pounds to become "grandma strong," I can't get it out of my head.

I can even picture the bread in the cute little yellow toaster we bought my mom for her birthday last year…it sits in the cabinet next to the jar of granola I made.

Granola: a breakfast or snack food consisting of rolled oats, nuts, honey, and brown sugar.

I derived my recipe from a bag of granola my bestie from Iowa gave me, which also consists of seeds, bits of dried fruit, wheat germ, molasses and other random items resting within mason jars in my cabinet.

Craving: a powerful desire for something.

Right now, I have a powerful craving for smushed avocado toast topped with dried cranberries, lightly toasted pine nuts, bits of granola…and just one piece will not do!

I abhor cravings. Or do I? Could it be that the craving for yummy food is a byproduct of the gift that God gave us to crave himself? As much as I am despising the one… I am not willing to remove it at the consequence of the other.

So here I sit…watching the sun rise, craving smushed avocado toast, with dried cranberries, lightly toasted pine nuts, bits of granola, and God.

Pondering in conflicted joy…

87, 72, and 76

If yesterday was "toast," today most certainly will be "cake," because we plan on having ourselves some celebratory birthday cake! Fried chicken, carrots, southern diced potatoes, and chocolate cake with chocolate frosting is what the birthday girl has requested, and that birthday girl is my mom!

I have partaken in about 72 percent of her life, my sister about 76 percent. That is a good percentage of time to both enrich and destroy a person's life.

I am the outdoorsy, outspoken, free spirit…while my sister is the indoorsy, internal, academic. My mom is all of those things. She loves mountains and fishing, books and movies and is pretty internal about her feelings…until she's not, and then she shoots right from the hip.

Proceeding from a good ponder… I concluded that she did not adjust to who my sister and I were, but gave us as many experiences and opportunities as possible for us to become who we were organically meant to be.

Mom always joyfully included our friends in all of those experiences, and still does. As a single mom, there was a lot she couldn't provide, but smothered us in a love that grew our confidence and ability to receive and give love to others.

As she turns eighty-seven today…she continues to exhibit who she is. One who is fearless in taking on technology and a smartphone. One who provides a piece of herself to her great grandchildren within crocheted blankets and animals, despite her rheumatoid arthritis. One who challenges her brain daily with word games, who still loves the outdoors, movies and books. Most particularly, she is one who continues to want to add more percentage points with her daughters.

I shall ponder…

May the Fourth/Force

Today, May the Fourth, is my daughter, and her husband's, first anniversary (Yes, they are *Star Wars* fans). Their first year of marriage was riddled with trials such as layoffs, a car accident, disability, job changes, and yes, with the COVID-19 quarantine.

However, when I look back at their first year, none of those things come into immediate focus, not even the quarantine deal-i-bob. When I focus in, I see a man who deeply loves his wife and a woman who deeply loves her husband. I see two individuals who desire to adventure and experience life as one, while still allowing the other to continue the growth of special friendships. I see two individuals serving Christ through youth ministry and their hearts desire to glorify Him, and yes, I see a bump of their love forming in my daughter's belly.

I am the product of a broken home. I know marriage can go wrong. It was painful when my parents divorced…it was also a relief.

There is the adage "Marriage is tough." After pondering, I take exception to that adage. I do! When I say marriage is tough… I am focusing on the tough. When I say it is easy, I am focusing on commitment, grace and respect…without exception…despite the tough.

So this morning, I prayed that marriage would be "easy" for Brad and Elise…full of commitment, grace, respect, and continued desire to serve, love, and glorify the Lord in their marriage and also in their growing family unit.

May the Fourth be with them…

I pondered…

Chirping

n., to utter a short, sharp, high-pitched sound.

Soooooo…there is this bird in the tree outside the window, by my sewing machine, that utters a short, sharp, high-pitched sound… once about every second…*for hours* at a time! It will stop for a short time, but begins again. It is aggravating, so I eventually tune it out with Beats in my ear and a podcast or music to drown over the sound. Birds behaving badly…indeed!

Then, I went to bed and was awakened by the utterance of a short, sharp, high-pitched chirp coming from the other side of the bedroom door. I didn't have to investigate… I knew the sound of a low battery signal from the CO alarm. I roamed in the dark with my bedhead hair and eyes three-fourths closed, from one green light on the ceiling to another trying to figure out which alarm was chirping. CO alarm behaving badly…indeed!

When my daughter lived at home… I owned a short, sharp constant chirp… I am sure perceived by my daughter as "high pitched aggravated-ness," to the tune of, is your bedroom clean, is your bedroom clean; is your homework done, is your homework done; don't text and drive, don't text and drive; be careful, be careful; what time will you be home, what time will you be home; did you feed the dog, did you feed the dog; don't text and drive, don't text and drive… Mom behaving lovingly…indeed!

The thing about chirping is, it has its purpose. It does. When its purpose is complete…with work…it can become a song…no longer requiring the listener to drown out the sound in some fashion.

What am I chirping about that needs to be turned into a song of patience, grace, love, and thankfulness? Am I chirping foolishly about the improper resting place of food items randomly placed in the back of shelves I cannot reach in the fridge? Or am I singing a song of thankfulness for the bounty it holds? Am I chirping about COVID-19? Or am I singing a song of protection and grace over those who must make decisions affecting large groups of people, and thankfulness that my family is healthy?

I do hear my chirping beat…

I shall ponder…

Cup

n., an open usually bowl-shaped drinking vessel.

I have said it before… I totally enjoy my morning cup of coffee. I also totally enjoy my afternoon cup of tea. I have a favorite "vessel" for my coffee and a favorite one for my tea…the two shall not be intertwined!

A cup can also be used to define the volume of ingredients it holds.

Psalm 23 speaks of how David's cup "runneth over" with goodness and mercy.

In Matthew 26, Jesus commands his disciples to "take the cup" and "drink," remembering blood shed for the forgiveness of sins.

Later on in Matthew 26, Jesus is in Gethsemane. He prays "My Father, if it be possible, let this cup pass from me; nevertheless, not as I will, but as you will."

One of my own most personal prayers is for the cup of chronic pain to be taken from me. I have an ongoing lesson in "learning" the importance of not negating the second part of that verse; "nevertheless, not as I will, but as you will."

I have ponderings bringing conclusions that the love of Christ most obviously would want to replace my Gethsemane cup with David's cup of goodness and mercy. Seems obvious right? But they are two different cups…not to be intertwined.

In one hand is David's cup of goodness and mercy. A cup measured in volume…always overflowing…following me wherever I go…unable to be emptied.

In the other hand is the Gethsemane cup I am meant to drink… the cup of remembrance for the blood shed for the forgiveness of sins and the cup of God's sovereign will. I am meant to drink it. I may seek God to take the cup of his will from me…however, he will likely work with me until I seek its removal to come only by helping me drink it instead.

I shall drink, and I shall ponder…

Arguments

n., an exchange of opposite views, with reasoning given to persuade others that an action or idea is wrong, often with heated or angry emotions.

Barry and I don't argue much. He admittedly will hang out forever in "discussion mode," but when heated or angry emotions are involved he goes into "survival mode," doing anything to end the argument while never admitting that he is wrong. (Barry agreed to this statement before "press time.")

Barry is not afraid to share heated or angry emotions with our daughter, however. Back in the day, they would argue loudly, saying whatever honest and hurtful words they needed to present their "argument." It would last about five minutes...then they would happily head out to share lunch or a Home Depot run. I was left alone in the bedroom painfully "pondering" the hurtful words. We are all such different creatures!

In preface to that... I also have been praying for PO through the Psalms. David and other Psalmists seem to argue quite a bit with God. Today, I hit a notation in my Bible about David's arguments with God...

"David wanted to be heard. He wanted safety. He desired godliness and he proposed to obtain those things through prayer" (John Piper).

The thing is, arguing in prayer with a timeless, sinless God is much different than arguing with a real-time partner in the midst of this world. Or is it?

I suppose the question is; do I want to win the argument or do I want to become more like Jesus? My first reaction is, I want both, which negates being more like Jesus...hmmmmmm.

I suspect I must caution myself when I feel I am "winning an argument," that I might also be the one acting least like Jesus. Another hmmmmm.

When deciding to cut my sinful losses short in "real-time" arguments… I am often left with those heated angry emotions. What to do… What to do… Well, Sandi, warrior for God…*take them to prayer*!

Are my emotions preceded by arrogance, pride, or constant annoying chirping? Am I pleading with God to make myself more joyful, more loving, more patient, more kind, more gentle, more humble, etc., etc., etc.?

I shall ponder…

Spinning

~~~~~~

n., the twisting technique where the fiber is drawn out, twisted, and wound in a circular motion onto a bobbin.

My head is twisting and spinning this morning. I have thoughts going in so many directions. I have taken each of them to prayer. My head is still spinning. I take the fact that my head is spinning to prayer, and continue to spin, it does.

My only choice is to review those things that I know. Those things that are greater than the things spinning in my head. The spinning eases, but resumes the second I shift my focus. Reality… I am not in heaven yet. Reality… I am living in a fallen world.

Sometimes our truths are heavy—whether our "reality" validates them or not. I am admitting…my reality does not validate my craziness!

Spinning anxiety seems to be fueled by the "what-ifs" in life. The reasonable assurance or "cure" for that anxiety is that everything is going to be okay. I sought scripture…

> And we know that for those who love God all things work together for good, for those who are called according to his purpose. Therefore I tell you, do not be anxious about your life, what you will eat, nor about your body, what you will put on. Instead, seek his kingdom, and these things will be added to you.

> Who shall separate us from the love of Christ? Shall tribulation, or distress, or persecution, or famine, or nakedness, or danger, or sword? I have said these things to you, that in me you may have peace. In the world you will have tribulation. But take heart; I have overcome the world. For all the promises of God find their Yes

in him. That is why it is through him that we utter our Amen to God for his glory. (Rom. 8:28; Luke 12:22, 12:31; Rom. 8:35; John 16:33; 2 Cor. 1:20)

Anxiety is not a sin…unless, of course, I make it a god. The command to "not be anxious" seems humanly impossible. Or is it?

If I believe the Bible's promises *"With man it is impossible, but not with God. For all things are possible with God"* (Mark 10:27).

I shall memorize scripture, and ponder…

God's Will

boule, grk, the sovereign, predetermined, inflexible decree of God.
thelema, grk, what is intended, commanded, morally just, and has movement when married with our own will.

Barry and I felt "led" to put our house up for sale…it is an unexplainable thing…the leading of the Holy Spirit, but it is real.

Besides the internal Holy Spirit thing…we received external confirmations in various ways…one being the "leading" came quite before the desire…another was that Barry and I were solidly together in this leading…there were more. However, comma, our house is still up for sale…not even *one* person has come through it since the quarantine.

This happening did not lead us to question the leading, but to dig deeper into what was the next step God may intend for us to take. After research, our realtor discovered that the only houses with "action" within our "Active Senior Adult Living Community" are homes that are "vacant." Seniors who are at higher risk are choosing not to visit occupied homes. Bummer.

What to do, what to do. Well, we prayed. We came up with a possible game plan and we desperately wanted to stay in the will of God within that game plan.

Moving to Vacaville could be God's *boule* road he has us providentially on, or it could be the *thelema* way we travel down that road…one that is married with our own will, but displays road signs of intention, direction, laws and commands. Only God knows at this point.

So where does that leave us? Back to prayer, and checking on the ease of opening doors…traveling down a road that will likely have many twists and turns, but will ultimately accomplish his *boule* will and hopefully his *thelema* will as well.

Oh, how I shall ponder…

Fast-Forward

n., used figuratively, is to shift one's attention or focus toward a later point in time quicker than normal speed.

Fast-forward... I use the term a lot...especially when telling a story.

Barry and I decide to move to Vacaville...fast-forward...house is up for sale and a steady pace of people come through...fast-forward... COVID-19 quarantine...fast-forward...get an offer on our house with a fifteen-day close, but due to the quarantine it falls apart...fast-forward...not one person comes through our home...fast-forward...we learn that home-buying seniors are choosing to only view vacant houses...fast-forward...we vacate our house and move into our RV...waiting for the next fast-forward...

The thing about fast-forward is, there is a lot of reshifting of "focus" that is not accounted for...the prayer, the conversations, the emotions, more prayer, the lists of positives and negatives, financial presentations, more emotions, more prayer, more prayer, decisions, more prayer, more prayer...

While a story can be told in fast-forward...the experience unquestionably cannot. When I choose to hit play on the mind-video-memory of a sunrise...assuredly, it will not be in fast-forward. I will remember the subtle changes in the sky. I will remember the geese flying overhead...the sounds of their call and the sound of their wings whipping back and forth in flight...the morning crow of the rooster I have named Reggie...the cows and sheep calling for their morning meal...the birds calling to each other, and again, the subtle changes in the sky.

Due to human impatience, fast-forward definitely has its place. But for now, I shall sit in "real time," drink up the subtle beauties of sound and sky...

And ponder...

Treasures

n., the accumulation of valuable items.

Recently, we became renters of a storage space that holds all of what I suppose could be considered our "nonessentials." I mean, if we can live without them on a daily basis…

I borrowed a sewing machine from my realtor, friend and cousin…who also took my "down" sewing machine to a reliable repair guy in her town. Sewing machine = essential. Realtor/friend/cousin = essential!

As I am direct with my words, I can also be direct with my decisions. Toss, save, toss, toss, toss, save. Those words equate to my new, most common phrase, bypassing my old standard, "It is, what it is."

The thing is, Barry is not quite as direct. His new, favorite word is "maybe."

There is this scripture that challenges me in such situations…

"Do not lay up for yourselves treasures on earth, where moth and rust destroy and where thieves break in and steal, but lay up for yourselves treasures in heaven, where neither moth nor rust destroys and where thieves do not break in and steal" (Matt. 6:19–21).

Even a decisive person has treasures on earth… I mean, is it heaven without a sewing machine, loads of silk and cotton fabric and threads, photo albums, collected pieces of art and more?

I am wondering if this verse is talking about our human nature's love of accumulation. Those things we buy that end up sitting on a shelf getting dusty, in the garage getting rusty and because we "might" use them someday, they have a powerful influence over us.

In the end, I think this verse may be more about our pleasure, which reveals our true treasures. I am becoming more and more aware of the "treasure" in simplicity. I am not there yet, but I am aware. If I put this "treasure" of awareness to glorifying work… I am laying it up in heaven.

In the meantime, I sure do have a lot of stuff in storage. Will I "regret" throwing some of it away? Or will I work toward a life of simplicity?

I shall ponder…

Tent

n., a collapsible shelter of fabric stretched and sustained by poles and used for a temporary dwelling.

We have headed out for a camping trip with an unspecified ending. Sounds scary and glorious at the same time. Definitely sounds "simple" (still pondering that one!).

I have been researching canopy screen rooms to provide bug and UV free protection outside our motor home. I wanted a floor attached to it. I guess I took it one step too far away from "simple" because *that* was not meant to be!

I found one that "seemed" perfect... UV protected, tightly meshed screen with a floor, and it goes up in less than sixty-six seconds! However, comma, its storage length is ten feet long!

This morning, as I stood in the rain, "drinking" in the sunrise... I thought about that tent...its purpose for portability and protection from the elements.

When I really took time to ponder... I realized that tent is me. I certainly am collapsible, and certainly both stretched and sustained by the poles of Christ...to be used as a temporary dwelling place for the Holy Spirit within me...meant to be enlarged by others who enter into my life...

Hmmmm... I shall ponder...

Vacancy

n., an empty or unoccupied space.

Since our "vacancy," we've had three couples view our unoccupied home space, and before we even got to our campsite...an offer.

I guess vacancy is a good thing if one is looking for a home during the pandemic, or a great pull-through campsite. It is easy to fill that space with personal "stuff" to quickly make it nonvacant.

The thing is, sometimes vacancy comes at a cost. Certainly the Israelites wandered in "vacancy," and Mary could not have been thrilled to find no vacant guest rooms while in labor.

Closer to home...we have all lost a loved one...that leaves a vacant spot in our hearts...a chair that holds the memory of a loved one who used to sit there...a dog bed that a pup use to play and rest in.

The Bible tells us before creation, the earth was formless, empty, vacant. It also tells us not to pray empty phrases that are vacant from the heart.

Where am I going with this? I don't know...let me take a moment to ponder and pray.

Sooo...the ponder here is not so much about vacancy, but what we fill a vacancy in our hearts, minds, activities, calendar, etc. with. Clearly the Bible has told us to set our minds on things that are above, not the things of the earth.

Could it be that hardness of heart locks the door to a vacant spot we can fill with those things from above? What are those things from above? Sincerity of heart? Simplicity? Perfect peace? That which is pure, noble, lovely, admirable, excellent praiseworthy? God's perspective? The Holy Spirit? Yes, the list goes on, and...

I shall ponder...

Regret

v.i., a feeling of sadness, repentance, or disappointment over something that has happened or been done.

I have been pondering regret for a bit now...despite the fact that my personal motto is "Live with Jesus; Live without regret."

I am adventurous and will try anything twice...food and experience. It has served me well; however, my regrets generally do not fall on what I eat, experience or even decisions made, but those that come from my mouth.

I seem to spend a lot of energy on what I "may" regret. Will I regret choosing to watch the reflection of the sunrise on our motor home instead of the deck? Will I regret the house that we choose to make our home? Will I regret the care and attention I gave my mom while she was living with us? None of which include what comes from my mouth.

Will I regret things I say to Barry as we make a new house our home? Will I regret things I say to my mom while we make our home hers? I need to learn from regrets of the past, and work on them in the present...not the future.

The thing is, Jesus died to cover over 10,000×10,000×10,000 regrets and whether they originate from my past, present, or future; I must let them lie with Him.

I shall ponder...

Contentment

n., the state of happiness and satisfaction

We all sat in total contentment as Barry and I DocuSigned our house into "contract." I'd like to say we were doing the same before the transaction began...back when we were living in our home and not one person had viewed it since the quarantine began. When we believed we were within God's will, but weren't "content" within that alone.

Why can't I be as content with promise as I am with resolve? Well, Sandi, that's a good question! I suppose it comes down to, yet again, control. I want to control how this transaction is going to go down...even worse... I want to control God and how he will work within it. Not a very spiritual thing to admit...

There is this scripture—often misrepresented—about being able to do all things through Christ who strengthens us (Phil. 4:11–13).

The thing is, that particular scripture is about being content whether in abundance or need—whether laying my head to sleep on a prison floor, motor home bed or in a home furnished with a fancy mechanical bed with a Tempurpedic mattress.

As we move forward in the purchase of a new home in Vacaville, California... I am challenged to be content...whether the perfect property, with the perfect home, becomes immediately available or not. When that perfect property and home does become available; I must be content whether its current owner chooses us to be its next owner, or not. Quite the challenge, whether in abundance or need, I can do all things through Christ who strengthens me, including "contentment."

I shall ponder...

Manzanita

n., any evergreen shrub or tree of the genus Arctostaphylos, having smooth red or orange bark and stiff, twisting branches.

There is a Manzanita tree outside our motor home door. It was so old that its dead parts were being wrapped with new growth that sheds every year about this time…revealing that beautiful and sturdy reddish bark underneath.

I couldn't help but make the connection to scripture…

"Therefore if anyone is in Christ, he is a new creation. The old has passed away; behold, the new has come." (2 Cor. 5:17).

So I had to ponder…what is this new creation? What does God see when he looks at me…an old, gnarly tree with new growth?

My Bible tells me that God sees me as a person of value…one who was fearfully and wonderfully made.

God sees me no longer a slave to sin and death, but one who is now righteous…victorious…saved by grace.

God sees me filled with His own Spirit…the author and perfecter of my faith.

God sees me in the midst of transformation…into the image of his Son.

God sees me as one who is to represent himself…one who is to walk in a manner worthy of his calling, a light to the world, both a witness and a worker, a citizen of heaven.

The thing is, that is not what "I" see when I look at this new, yet still gnarly creation. I focus on the one part that has not yet shown its new red, sturdy, beautiful skin. I have not stepped back and taken a look at my entire "being" as God sees me. Starting with the knowledge that I am a person of value…one who was fearfully and wonderfully made.

I have a lot to ponder…

Simplicity Of Stuff

phrase, "An inward attitude reflected in an outward lifestyle" (Richard Foster).

What is that inward attitude? An attitude that is less reactive and more intentional? An attitude steeped with humbleness? An attitude that acknowledges all we have is a gift from God? An attitude that first seeks the Kingdom of God?

So what will that outer lifestyle look like? I'm not sure, but I am certain it is not found on shopyourwayintooblivion.com. I am certain it is not found in some of the stuff I fill my brain with…you know, personal, political and even spiritual… Who did it… Who should have done it… How they should have done it…that constant noise that has nothing to do with seeking first the Kingdom of God.

Let me be clear…as I am even typing this… I am challenged… convicted…in this area. There is the stuff I need to remove from my life…stuff I don't want to remove from my life…even stuff I am not willing to remove from my life…at least at this point.

One of my convictions is that anything I am grouping into the word *stuff,* needs to be considered.

"Simplicity" has a name…an important name and I will keep it a ponder in the forefront of my mind, because that IS where it belongs, because it provides opportunity to connect with what is most important in my life…what is most important to God.

I shall continue to ponder…

Reflections

n., a response to a particular stimulus.

There is something so beautiful about reflections…especially if they are of large, grown pines nesting in a mountainside.

What came to my pondering this morning…as I looked at the reflections of such trees from the window by my bed…were personal reflections.

The thing about personal reflections are, they are an opportunity, an opportunity that can be met with a deep form of learning power, with a fresh perspective, with new opinions, with criticism, or for me, in a more artistic form that captures all of the above.

If I could see the reflection "real time" of what I am saying or doing, how would that impact my response? I suppose it would have to do with the "stimulus." Was the stimulus my carnal, self-serving nature, or was it the selfless nature of Christ?

As I reflect… I still see an artistic impression that captures both. Maybe that truly is the beauty of reflection.

I know one artistic impression I have is our daughter. Her portrait has come to life with the brush stroke of many, and I am thankful to all who have participated.

I know one artistic impression I have is my walk with Christ. It is not all pretty pastels with soft strokes…more of a weird abstract… that seems to make no sense…except to the artist…who has deemed it valuable, and for that I am also thankful.

I shall reflect, and ponder…

Peace

n., to be complete and sound.

A perfect house came on the market…at a lower price than we expected. We quickly put in an offer…as have others. We possibly won't know who the new, lucky, chosen owner of the home is until the end of the weekend. Oddly, I am "currently" at peace.

I had to ponder this because the adjective that normally describes me in such situations is not peaceful, but anxious, inpatient, unsettled. So where did this wondrous "peace" come from? I am thinking trust. Proverbs 3:5–6 says:

> Trust in the LORD with all your heart,
> and do not lean on your own understanding.
> In all your ways acknowledge him,
> and he will make straight your paths.

Truth be told…if we had not gone through a pandemically lengthy sell of our home, a move with our "stuff" in storage and us in our motor home, to the inescapable beauty of the mountains that has very limited cellage and no TV…peace may have evaded me.

It seems the Lord took me on a path requiring trust, and at the end of it…was peace. Hmmmmm, so much to ponder here.

Am I trusting the LORD with "all" my heart? Clearly, I am not. I am trying… I am on a straight path of trust until anxiety, or the like, takes hold. I then veer off to a winding path that does not veer back onto the straight path until I again, "trust."

Am I leaning on my own understanding? Actually, it's one of my favorite pastimes! It seems difficult to separate God's wisdom from my understanding. Maybe I am not supposed to. I just searched my Bible and Proverbs alone speaks highly of "not" separating my understanding from my faith, but encourages it.

So what's the deal-i-bob? I am thinking it is more about not allowing my understanding to draw me to conclusions...conclusions based on my imperfect perceptions.

Where does that leave me? It leaves me acknowledging God... putting my imperfect understanding into the hands of a perfect God...trusting Him, and finding my way back to a straight path, which leads to peace.

I shall continue to ponder...

The Climb

On May 29, 1953, Edmund Hillary and Tenzing Norga became the first explorers to reach the 29,035' summit of Mount Everest, the highest point on earth.

I do understand a call to the high point of a mountain, but I don't feel the need to ponder doing such a thing. What strikes me is both the preparation and knowledge needed to experience such a wonder…especially knowing those who tried before you weren't successful.

Without those unsuccessful experiences, Hillary and Norgay surely wouldn't have been able to accomplish their feat. Those unsuccessful experiences brought necessary knowledge needed for eventual success.

The first recorded attempt was made in 1921 by a group who made it four hundred miles up the mountain when a raging storm forced their return. Before the descent one of the explorers, George Mallory, saw what appeared to be a feasible route up the peak. I doubt this observation was celebrated.

The thing is, none of us want to be "unsuccessful," offering only knowledge. We would much rather be the successful one who brings celebration.

Would I rather be the one who is celebrated by achievements, reputation and blessings or would I rather be the one who is tried with struggles and suffering? My outer, human self would rather have celebration and blessing. However, my inner, spiritual self, struggles with the knowledge that anything that draws me closer to God, is the greatest blessing, and celebrated by God Himself.

I have experienced both struggles and suffering. They have both, in fact, brought me closer to God. Am I "woman enough" to celebrate those struggles and suffering? Sure, when they are over and done with. But what about celebrating the suffering of chronic pain that lingers on…

I shall ponder...as I trek up my mountain...learning, gaining knowledge about what truly offers me spiritual confidence and makes me unshakable. Who I can lean on when a storm comes and I am no longer able to take steps forward...those who will carry me... learning, within failure, true blessing can be found, and always rests in God, Himself.

I shall ponder...

Frustration and Peace

Frustration: *n.,* the feeling of being upset or annoyed, especially because of the inability to change or achieve something.

Peace: *n.,* a state of tranquility or quiet.

Yesterday started with me strongly inclining Barry that we should move from our current campsite to another (still beautiful but on a concrete pad) because several thunder storms were due to come through. After a good "discussion" we moved to the concrete "Cliff" area...no dirt...also, almost no cellage. Ughhh...

When we did get a whiff of cellage...we received a text from our realtor that there are at least nine offers on the table for the house we also bid on, and they aren't reviewing offers for several more days. Ughhh...

I could have remained on the straight path of peace, as I drew the mountain scenes I saw before me on my iPad, but I was much more compelled to veer off onto that dark, winding path of frustration. I was determined to find a way to both change and achieve something...becoming upset and annoyed because I couldn't. I even had a "discussion" with God...challenging him that maybe both his timing and plan for us was askew. Ughhh...

Even more frustrating was the constant replaying of some of the words I had written previously about "peace." Ughhh...

When I actually went back and read that post... I was bonked on the head with the inspired words of God...

> *Trust in the LORD with all your heart,*
> *and do not lean on your own understanding.*
> *In all your ways acknowledge him,*
> *and he will make straight your paths.* (Prov. 3:5–6)

I did "eventually" get back on the straight road of peace... food was involved...trust was involved...not leaning on my own understanding was involved...not dissecting my past frustration was involved, and acknowledging a sovereign God was definitely involved...

I shall ponder...

Humbleness

n., having or showing a modest or low estimate of one's own importance.

We had *quite* the rain, flash flood, thunder, hail storm yesterday. Luckily, the wind that was blowing the "said storm" in, caused us to take down our cano-tent-opy (a tent with a floor, lots of big, zippered windows and room for chairs, footstools, dog beds, a sewing machine table and *no* mosquito's or bee's) before the storm came in.

Anyway, we were all glad we sacrificed cellage for a concrete floor. I again found myself having two paths to consider…the straight path of humbleness, or the crooked path of "I told you so-ness." Because I am going "public" I will take the straight path to humbleness.

There is a lot to ponder about humbleness: "the act of" vs. "being." Clearly if my "being" was humble…the decision to put into action humbleness would be unnecessary. I am thinking, however, those "actions" are necessary steps on the straight path to humbleness.

Another thing I ponder about humbleness is dissecting who "I" say I am from who "Christ" says I am. It seems like it should be easy to figure out, but sometimes I forget who I am listening to.

A new character enters, standing on the other side of the hedge that separates the straight path from the dark and windy one, "the evil one" who likes to "lie, cheat, and steal." The one who lies about my value in Christ, who tells me my value is shown by the pricy "stuff" I own. The one who tells me my identity lies in the shape of my body and the tally board of successes I can keep. The one who enjoys cheating me from peace, joy and unconditional love. The one who wanted to steal my eternity with God by telling me I could do it all on my own. The one who encourages me to walk toward the land of "I told you so-ness."

Scripture tells us not to waste time pondering the evil one.

I shall ponder an opposite…humbleness…

Motherhood

n., the state or experience of having or raising a child; an expression of the character and nature of God.

Motherhood is not a hobby, but a calling. It is not what we make time for, but what God gave us time for.

Motherhood is a mission field. Not a mission field in an intriguing faraway place where our supporters are informed of our wondrous activity and progress through a monthly newsletter. It is a mission field where our wondrous activity and progress is measured through the demonstration of our strong-willed child at the grocery check-out counter, a tired child at the zoo, a bored child at the restaurant dinner table. The list goes on. Motherhood is the most visible and highly criticized mission field on the planet.

However, comma, motherhood is the most intimate, hands on mission work that can ever be sacrificed for the sake of the gospel.

"*Train up a child in the way he should go; even when he is old he will not depart from it*" (Prov. 22:6).

Easier said than done. It seems easier to motivate our children to go on a mission trip to that faraway place than to motivate them to load the dishwasher. That seemingly impossible task of teaching them to care for their home environment and their siblings is the mission work that prepares them to go out into the world as disciples. Our most important motherhood work…is teaching our children the importance of "being" a disciple of Christ.

When my daughter graduated from college, she gifted us with a wall hanging she made…it has the words "Every life I'll touch, you'll touch as well." That is a true expression of mother/parenthood. As mothers, we need to look at our children in faith, who they have the potential to become, and how many people will be ministered to because of the ministry we are pouring into them.

Motherhood, the most precious ministry I have ever been honored with and called too. Soon, a new ministry will begin for me…it is called grandma-hood. Never to be confused with motherhood, but with the same purpose and importance of expressing the nature of God.

I shall ponder…

New Beginning

adj., having recently come into existence: recent.

There were a total of eighteen offers for the house we bid on. Ours was not the offer they chose to work with. The number 18 represents "bondage" in the Bible.

Yesterday, I received eight text messages from people encouraging me through their earnest prayers. It was 8:00 p.m. last night when our realtor texted that our offer was not chosen. The number 8 represents a new beginning or new order in the Bible.

The straight and windy path analogy continues on as a current "theme" for me. I can choose to walk the dark and windy path of bondage...or...the straight path heading toward a new beginning. With help from the earnest prayers of those eight people, I am walking the straight path toward a new beginning...in peace. Maybe not "perfect peace" but definitely in peace.

My ponders tell me that because I am not able to see our new "home" in the distance, does not mean I must step over that hedge onto that dark and windy path of bondage. The evil one tells me I must, but the earnest prayers of many encourage me I must not.

I gaze up from my typing and see the words "home is where you park it" above our door. If there is one thing I have learned about campers, it's that we like to make campsites our homes. It may be the addition of twinkle lights, a canopy/cano-tent-opy, or a firepit circled with used camping chairs fashioned with duct tape repairs, s'more droplets and drenched with many camping memories.

What seems to be of most importance in making a campsite a home, is the placement of that heavy camp table and bench. It seems every new camper determines that it must be placed in a new position (it's not just us!). The perfect placement may be several feet to the right or left or clear across the campsite, but where we play cards and eat our meals seems to be integral in what makes a campsite our home.

So off we go in a few days to our new glampsite home (with cellage, free Wifi, and cable TV!) along the Delta to "officially" close down our Rio Vista home. We will be heading toward a new beginning or order…where the sun continues to rise…

and I will continue to ponder…

Path

n., a trodden track or way.

Today we head from the Donner Pass area back to Rio Vista to close out the sale of our home. During our stay in Donner Pass we encountered warmth, cold, rain, hail, thunder and lightning, and warm weather again. It is mind boggling that we are now planning a travel route on back highways and roads to avoid traveling on a major interstate through the Sacramento Valley where riots broke out.

Soooo…the thing about the straight vs windy and dark path… is that the straight path may have turbulence to head through. God will guide us through that turbulence… He is the stability under our feet.

When I find myself encountering turbulent twists and turns while on my sanctification journey, the first thing I should do is seek God. Is it God's sure foundation that is under my feet? Have I veered off His foundation? Is it an opportunity to trust God when I am certain his foundation is under my feet yet turbulence and sorrow comes? Am I leaning on my own understanding or "perception" of what such "turbulence" means? Are the certainties of Christ good enough to overrule the uncertainties of life?

So much to ponder on my long ride home.

Full Joy

"Christian joy is a good feeling in the soul, produced
by the Holy Spirit, as he causes us to see the beauty
of Christ in the word and in the world."

—John Piper

I traveled about fifty yards from our RV…in the car…in my PJs…
with my cup of coffee…to reunite with my Rio Vista sunrise. It was,
complete and utter, full joy…a feeling deep down in my soul. I didn't
need my sunrise deck…it turns out… I only needed the Holy Spirit.

What a challenge…to cease expecting joy to be created in places,
people, or things, but by the hand of the Holy Spirit.

I have had a similar feeling while walking down Main Street
USA in Disneyland. Could it be that joy is not in "the place," but
my relinquishment of all personal stresses and responsibilities at the
entrance gate? Maybe that relinquishment is what allows me to discover that place deep down in my soul where such gifts are found.

What other gifts are found in that deep place? Certainly, love,
joy, peace, patience, kindness, goodness, faithfulness, gentleness, and
self-control. Such a good gift…fruit…to consume.

The thing is, joy is a part of "one" fruit…with joy comes the rest
of the fruit. If I am not willing to partake in any of the other parts

of the fruit…say patience or self-control… The Theology of Sandi finds it likely that the ones we desire will also be out of sight.

As I head to my Bible to seek more understanding, I find "joy" both simple and complex. Here is the simple:

"*These things* (speaking about the vine and the branches) *I have spoken to you, that my joy may be in you, and that your joy may be full*" (John 15:11).

His full "joy" is in me! The complex part seems to be uncovering it and letting it be free.

I shall ponder…

The Holy Spirit

n., the third Person of the Trinity through whom God acts, reveals His will, empowers individuals, and discloses His personal presence in the Old and New Testament.

Several days ago, Barry and I prepared to go house hunting. We had appointments for three properties. We "DocuSigned" all the necessary COVID-19 paperwork, had masks, foot coverings, and gloves in hand. Right before we left, Barry found a new property that came up on the market that interested him. We did a quick, but COVID appropriate last-minute addition to our tour.

The first two properties were "fine" but there was absolutely no sense of "home" for me.

The third property had an amazing front yard, raised bed garden that meandered beautiful flowers through vegetables. The inside was quaint with beautiful, well maintained, original hardwood flooring...lots of recessed lighting and windows that overlooked more beautiful flowers, plants, and trees. The kitchen had just been remodeled, and there was a "sun room" perfect for my sewing and art. Definitely, move-in ready. I think I heard the angels sing...

The fourth property was an old, small, farmhouse on an acre of land. The house was a small version of the Winchester Mystery House near where I grew up in San Jose. It was my least favorite of the four properties. Not move-in ready. We'll leave it at that.

Barry and I are usually on the same page... I assumed he heard the angels sing on property 3. To my horror, he heard the angels sing on property 4. Are you kidding me? Angels were not present on property 4!

What to do... Clearly, it is not the character of the Holy Spirit to lead a married couple in two separate directions. As a Christian, I prayed, and asked for the leading of the Holy Spirit.

What I know is...

The book of John tells us we receive the Holy Spirit by faith, he dwells within us, helps, teaches, guides, reminds, and comforts us.

The book of Ephesians tells us we are sealed, filled, equipped, commanded to walk, be led, bear fruit, live and keep in step with the Spirit.

The book of Galatians says he bears his fruit through us.

Acts says he empowers us....

I shall ponder...truly ponder...

Silence

n., the absence of sound; stillness.

God has been silent. His presence has been incapsulating, but his leading has not evolved. I have asked him many questions, but he was silent, or was I hearing impaired?

The thing about claiming God is silent…is to negate all of the truth and promises he has already spoken…it is to negate his Inspired Word… *Ouch!*

In a rare moment of "quiet, aloneness" in the RV…normally filled with three humans and two pups (we have taught to think they are human), I searched the Word.

"Draw near to God, and he will draw near to you." Check!

"For God alone my soul waits in silence…my hope is from him" Hmmmm…

My soul is to wait in silence. I believe God still wants to hear my questions…it draws me near to him, but it is my soul that is to wait in silence.

My soul is that part of me that is eternal…that is made by God, for God, and to need God. The part of me that has truly acknowledged Christ as my Savior.

Could it be that it is in my soul I find perfect faith, perfect peace, perfect anything? A place that doesn't need to have questions answered? Certainly it would do me well to "wait" in that place.

In the meantime, the reality outside of that "place" is still before me. My questions to God still come. Where do you want us to live? What stipulations are we to surrender in order for us to find a house? What really matters in finding a property to call home?

What I learned through scripture…despite God's outward silence…is that he values unity. That it is not so much where I lay my head, but that I don't allow a wedge to come between my husband and I in the process of finding it.

"For God alone my soul waits in silence…my hope is from him." Check!

I shall surrender, I shall ponder…in silence…

The Dance

v.i., to move one's body rhythmically usually to music.

We made a bid on another home in Vacaville. Now the dance begins. That awkward time in real estate when both buyer and seller rally to a middle ground in price, inspection work, and apparently even much more.

The thing about the real estate dance is, both sides are doing a different dance...to different music, yet a common, compromising, beat must be found...the beat of "money."

I have never needed music to dance around the house...do it often...have enough music in my head for a personal opus. But outward music certainly helps...providing a mathematical count...a science behind it all.

My daughter use to dance on a competitive team...they placed highest when each member danced the same moves, at the same time. Lots of practice and money was involved in making that happen.

Of course, this led me to a spiritual ponder of questions. Am I dancing the same dance as the Lord? Have I gone off beat to the music in my own head? Is the poetry of The Word my music? Am I trying to find a compromising beat with the Lord...mixing my music, my intentions with his? Am I practicing to stay in beat with Him through knowledge of who He is, how He moves? Am I willing to sacrifice all I own...including a home...to find His beat?

I shall ponder...

Gravity and Inertia

n., while inertia is a resistance of any physical object to any change in its state of motion, gravity is a curvature of spacetime attracting uneven distribution of masses together.

On Earth, gravity gives weight to physical objects, and the Moon's gravity causes the ocean tides.

Mathematically speaking, $F=Gm_1m_2/r_2$, where G is called the gravitational constant. It has a value of $6.6726\times10\text{-}11$ m3 kg-1 s-2. (I copied that from NASA's website... I am *not* that smart.)

While Barry and I moved our possessions into storage...we certainly felt the effects of gravity...no math needed. A large TV is much easier to slide into the back of a car...than get down from a cove over the fireplace.

Gravity, we don't truly know what it is, but we do know its effects.

Gravity may cause the beautiful upward dance of the waves, but man's upward force against gravity can cause a bloody mess atop a bald man's head when said head bashes into a piece of metal...twice. (Polysporen and a Band-Aid resolved the effects).

Theology of Sandi: While "G" may equal the gravitational constant in math, "G" certainly equals the gravitational constant of God in my spiritual life. At a certain point in our lives, G=God commands our attention and asks us to view the invisible with the same attention and "weight" as we have previously viewed the physical world. He attracts us, and when we try to defy spiritual gravity, and attract Him...a bloody mess happens (Polysporen and a Band-Aid *not* resolving the effects).

There is also the law of inertia which states that things that are at rest require far more energy to get moving than things which are already in motion. Spiritual Inertia: *ouch!* Prayer, reading my Bible, doing that which I know God wants me to do...is movement...even if I am in a spiritual dry spell.

Science… I have always enjoyed it, and have never been afraid of it. It has given me great insight into God… His order of the world… His order of my spiritual life. Spiritual Gravity… Spiritual Inertia… I shall ponder…

Spiders

~~~~~~

n., an eight-legged predatory arachnid which injects poison into their prey, and most kinds spin webs in which to capture insects.

Soooo…where do I begin? Let's underline the fact that spiders are predatory insects!

Early this morning, as Barry was leaving to finalize the closure of our Rio Vista home… I mentioned the stupidity of trying to get my morning coffee going without my glasses on. We laughed, he left. A bit later, while pouring my coffee, with my glasses on, I noticed a nasty spider on a small, but *full* spiderweb just to the side of the coffee maker…

Now, there are certain laws within the Hall households; they have been discussed and adopted, such as, one must enter Disneyland from the right tunnel, or if a husband is present, he must kill a household spider. Oh, man—missed opportunity!

With my mom sleeping peacefully on a bed just feet away… I knew I had to woman up and extinguish said spider. A short prayer was said. A photo was taken as evidence. A wet, blue, Scotch-Brite absorbent wipe was chosen as the murder weapon. A sandwich baggie was chosen as a grave.

Traumatized… I sent Barry a photo of the victim before its demise. Such a precious man…offered to turn around and come back to the motor home to fulfill the Hall man's law…even though he hadn't been present. I told him I "Hall-manned up." He was impressed.

Spiders didn't use to concern me…until… I was bitten by a brown recluse. It caused horrid sickness and pain. Yes, I am no longer a fan.

If there is a spiritual thought here…it is the predatory, Evil One's spidery web he tries to capture believers in…we may get tangled up in the web…he may bite…we may even encounter trauma ensuring the demise of his plan for us, but we will remain victorious!

I shall ponder…

Noodle

n., a narrow, ribbonlike strip of dough, usually made of flour, eggs, and water. A cylindrical piece of polyethylene foam, useful when learning to swim, for floating, for rescue reaching, water play, and for aquatic exercise.

The RV park we are staying in has a swimming pool. Following appropriate COVID rules…reservations were made for 2:00–3:00 p.m. I grabbed the Dollar Tree pool noodle Barry and I had purchased to secure safety for bonking heads when our RV's awning was extended.

My daughter and I gleefully headed for the pool…she, with the heaviness of thirty-two weeks of pregnancy…me with the heaviness of packing and moving household items against "gravity and inertia."

The noodle was thrown into the pool. I had exaggerated visions of floating luxuriously, pretending I was holding an icy cold Arnold Palmer in my hand. Somehow in that vision the noodle transformed into a full floating chez lounge with an umbrella and a body fit for the runway. As I removed my shorts…reality set in. I needed to maneuver my swimming skills to secure ownership of the one noodle that had floated to the middle of the pool.

One toe in the water changed the entire scope of the hour. The water was *freezing*! No heater, no solar panels were found. The noodle slowly and randomly continued to float with the breeze. My daughter and I sat on the side of the pool with our feet partially immersed in the cold water and began a great conversation.

Eventually, we stood and began to travel down the steps very slowly…maybe one step every fifteen minutes…the great conversation continued to flow. The noodle continued to float ever so peacefully.

At the end of the hour, neither of us had fully immersed our bodies, but a great conversation was had. No noodle needed. Or was it? Was it the thought of floating weightlessly on a noodle that drew me to a private, secure and peaceful place where an intimate conversation was had?

I shall ponder…

God's Will and Mercy

God's Will: boule, grk, the sovereign, predetermined, inflexible decree of God.

God's Will: thelema, grk, what is intended, commanded, morally just, and has movement when married with our own will.

Mercy: n., unmerited favor.

I have been pondering quite a bit about God's will. What His will is for me in any given situation.

Through many long ponders… I have come to the conclusion… I have no idea.

What I have concluded…is that I spend far too much time pondering what I don't know about God's will…instead of what I do know.

There is this chapter in the Bible; I have memorized it twice… still have "most" of it memorized. It begins with information about God's will for me…for man.

"I appeal to you therefore, brothers, by the mercies of God, to present your bodies as a living sacrifice, holy and acceptable to God, which is your spiritual worship. Do not be conformed to this world, but be transformed by the renewal of your mind, that by testing you may discern what is the will of God, what is good and acceptable and perfect" (Rom. 12:1–2).

Romans 12 first encourages me to live by the mercies of God. The word "mercy" comes from both the Hebrew and Greek term "hesed." I read an entire book on "hesed," it is one of those words that is accurately indefinable, but the closest inaccurate definition rallies around God's lovingkindness. His lovingkindness when I am blowing it…when I am not showing mercy to others…yes, the list goes on…for miles.

Farther down in Romans 12 I am given examples. I like examples…until I am called to live them out. Paul doesn't tell me to just show mercy, but to do it with cheerfulness. I can do that. I can also "not" do that; it is actually quite easy.

Paul continues his examples of mercy by encouraging us to let our love be genuine...to be generous to our fellow believer's...to bless those who persecute us...to weep with those who weep...to associate with those we don't necessarily want to associate with...to repay no one evil for evil...to feed the hungry...

Am I putting the mercies of God on display for the world to see? Am I putting the mercies of God on display for no one, except God, to see?

I shall ponder...

God's Will: A Living Sacrifice

God's Will: boule, grk, the sovereign, predetermined, inflexible decree of God.
God's Will: thelema, grk, what is intended, commanded, morally just, and has movement when married with our own will.
Living sacrifice: the total surrender of one's best to God.

Still pondering God's will...

"I appeal to you therefore, brothers, by the mercies of God, to present your bodies as a living sacrifice, holy and acceptable to God, which is your spiritual worship. Do not be conformed to this world, but be transformed by the renewal of your mind, that by testing you may discern what is the will of God, what is good and acceptable and perfect" (Rom. 12:1–2).

▶ God's will for me is to both receive and give mercy.
▶ God's will for me is to present my body as a living sacrifice.

God's will for me is to present my body as a living sacrifice. How many times have I read this...heard it in a song, but what does it really mean? Quite the ponder.

I suppose I should start with an OT definition of sacrifice. "The ritual through which the Hebrew people offered the blood or the flesh of an animal to God as a 'substitute payment' for their sin." Man did not come up with the idea... God did.

The NT book of Hebrews, tells us that sacrifices, in themselves, had no value or efficiency. They were only the "shadow of good things to come," pointing a worshipper forward to the coming of the great High Priest, who, in the fullness of the time, "was offered once and for all to bear the sin of many." In steps Christ...a "perfect" example of a living sacrifice.

I can only begin my walk as a living sacrifice to God through my profession of faith, my profession of the Gospel story, my profession that Christ is my personal Savior.

But what does it look like to continue that walk as a living sacrifice to God?

- ~ A living, working, constant dedication of myself, and my best, to God.
- ~ A death or total surrender of those things that do not bring glory to God.
- ~ Suffering is likely to be involved.
- ~ The suffering, the sacrifice, is not to atone for sin but to bring worship to God, to the Great "I Am," who offered his Son, who once and for all, gave His life as a Savior, to atone for my sin, and the sins of many.

I shall ponder…

God's Will: Holiness

God's Will: boule, grk, the sovereign, predetermined, inflexible decree of God.

God's Will: thelema, grk, what is intended, commanded, morally just, and has movement when married with our own will.

Holiness: n., "God's infinite value as the absolutely unique, morally perfect, permanent person that he is and who by grace made himself accessible—his infinite value as the absolutely unique, morally perfect, permanent person that he is" (John Piper).

- ► God's will for me is to both receive and give mercy.
- ► God's will for me is to present my body as a living sacrifice.
- ► God's will for me is holiness.

Holiness means "to be set apart." This applies to places where God is present, like the Temple and the Tabernacle, and to things and persons related to those holy places or to God Himself.

It also means to be perfect, transcendent, or spiritually pure. This applies primarily to God, but secondarily to saints or godly people.

Those definitions sent me to so many places in my Bible... I continually lost track of what my original focus was.

John Piper's definition of holiness is, indeed, scholarly and well thought out, but what does it mean for "me" to be called to holy living. I must fully understand, as much as I can, to pursue God's will.

God is set apart as unique, transcendent, and spiritually pure. God has made himself accessible to me through Christ's atonement on the cross. It is the only way I can pursue God's will of holiness. God considers me righteous because He counts Jesus' goodness instead of my sins...through my profession of faith in Christ.

I am becoming holy through the "continual," sanctifying work of the Holy Spirit in me. This process requires "continual" obedient submission.

God's will for me is continual, obedient submission to the process; to do what is right, what is glorifying to God.

I shall ponder…

God's Will: Conformation

God's Will: *boule, grk,* the sovereign, predetermined, inflexible decree of God.

God's Will: *thelema, grk,* what is intended, commanded, morally just, and has movement when married with our own will.

Conformation: *n.,* taking on the same form or shape.

- ▶ God's will for me is to both receive and give mercy.
- ▶ God's will for me is to present my body as a living sacrifice.
- ▶ God's will for me is holiness.
- ▶ God's will for me is to not be conformed to this world.

I live in the world. I truly enjoy that which God has created and placed in this world for me to enjoy…sunrises that are new every morning…the mountains (Yosemite) with its rock formations and uncountable amounts of the color green and ever-present smell of pines…the US coastlines that display both the power and tranquility of the ocean.

I would be evading a full truth if I did not also admit that I truly enjoy man made fabric and silk threads I have collected during our travels…a (Go Giants) baseball game…a bag or two of salt-and-vinegar Kettle Chips and definitely more than two pairs of comfy shoes and perfectly designed purses!

My first ponder took me to the difference between conformed and transformed. Both of them require change, submission and someone or something else as a standard of measure.

Almost illegibly in my Bible is a note I had written in the 1980s: "Conformation comes from the outside in… Transformation comes from the inside out."

So what does it look like to be conformed to this world?

My ponders challenge me that while having a room full of fabric and thread is not conformation to the world, looking for joy there, instead of the Lord, is. Attending or watching a baseball game is not conformation to the world…as long as it doesn't keep me from doing or being what the Lord desires.

So the thing is (remembering holiness), separation vs. participation. I can "participate" as long as it doesn't cause me to separate from that sanctification process…

I shall ponder…

God's Will: Transformation

God's Will: *boule, grk,* the sovereign, predetermined, inflexible decree of God.

God's Will: *thelema, grk,* what is intended, commanded, morally just, and has movement when married with our own will.

Transformation: *n.,* a complete change in the appearance or character of something or someone, especially so that that thing or person is improved.

- ▶ God's will for me is to both receive and give mercy.
- ▶ God's will for me is to present my body as a living sacrifice.
- ▶ God's will for me is holiness.
- ▶ God's will for me is to not be conformed to this world.
- ▶ God's will for me is to be transformed.

I looked up the Greek meaning of the word transform. Interestingly enough, it is the root word for metamorphosis. It is the word used in Scripture for the transfiguration of Christ…when Christ's *"face shone like the sun, and his clothes became white as light."*

So my 1980, almost illegible, Bible note takes on an even greater meaning. Could it be that conformation comes from man and transformation comes from God?

Transformation appears not to be switching from the checklist of the law…to the checklist of the fruit of the Spirit. For example, it seems there is quite the difference between "displaying" kindness and "being" kind. God's will for me begins with displaying kindness… then transforms me into a kind person.

I take great pause because this seems like an undoable task. Or is it? If transformation comes from God, then it appears I am off the hook. Or am I? There is that "next" part of the sentence, *"but be transformed by the renewal of your mind."*

Soooo I take it; my job is the renewal of my mind, which seems to be more than avoiding all kinds of ungodly behaviors, but taking on godly behaviors, such as the fruit of the Spirit.

Soooo, through my commitment to "acts" of Godly behaviors... God transforms me. Through my commitment to know God through the Scriptures... God transforms me. Through my commitment to communicate with God through prayer... God transforms me. Through my commitment to do the will of God... God transforms me.

One day...on the other side of heaven... I will be completely transformed...not just a body without pain, but a bright light.

I shall ponder...

God's Will: Discernment

God's Will: *boule, grk,* the sovereign, predetermined, inflexible decree of God.

God's Will: *thelema, grk,* what is intended, commanded, morally just, and has movement when married with our own will.

Discernment: *n.,* the ability to decide between truth and error, right and wrong.

- ▶ God's will for me is to both receive and give mercy.
- ▶ God's will for me is to present my body as a living sacrifice.
- ▶ God's will for me is holiness.
- ▶ God's will for me is to not be conformed to this world.
- ▶ God's will for me is to be transformed.
- ▶ God's will for me is discernment.

The thing about discernment is, "testing" is involved…not a fan. I get it. As I walk in this sanctification process… I am called to tighter discernment. Once I have passed the test of "right and wrong or truth and error" come the tests in that gray area, distinguishing between good, better, and best…loose vs. solid and biblically accurate.

I often walk through these tests…had a day of it yesterday, but in the end I am not certain of my "grade." I know I didn't get an A+… I know I didn't get a F-.

Scripture tells me it is through these tests I will *know*… Hmmmmm…am I more worried about what I learned from the test? Or more worried about the grade? You know…once the test is complete…the grade is given…the skill lies dormant in a grading book somewhere. I am thinking this is not God's will.

This "good, better, best, solid and biblically accurate" discernment I obtain best proves its worth when I put it into practice. The more testing…the more practice…the tighter my discernment will become.

So what about yesterday? As I ponder… I realize that if I look at the day as one SAT test… I may get into "spiritual" college, but am definitively not earning a scholarship. However, if I look at the day through the many individual quizzes… I can best "discern" "*the will of God, what is good and acceptable and perfect.*"

I shall ponder…

Chosen

v., having been selected as the best or most appropriate.

Our offer on a house, a home, was chosen and accepted! Celebrate with me here! Can I hear a *woot woot?* Can I see a happy dance? Anyone want to pop a "can" of the bubbly with me?

House #1 did not choose us. House #2, theoretically, did not choose us because we were the only offer…little did we know at the time…it was for a good reason. House #3 chose us as the best or most appropriate.

The Bible tells us of many instances of choosing…such as:

God chose Moses as a leader and Saul, David, and Solomon as kings.

God chose Abraham, Israel as His chosen people, and Jerusalem as a place of habitation and worship.

God chose Christ, a servant, the one whom He upholds, and in whom His soul delights.

Christ chose his Apostles.

Christ chose me…to do good work for Him, to glorify Him and to live with Him in eternity.

My faith did not choose Christ, but is a result of God's grace in choosing me. (Theological belief of Sandi.)

"But you are a chosen race, a royal priesthood, a holy nation, a people for his own possession, that you may proclaim the excellencies of him who called you out of darkness into his marvelous light" (1 Pet. 2:9).

I was chosen by God… I am speechless. We were chosen by owners of a home we will move into…in about thirty days…we are ecstatic!

I shall ponder the joy…

Purpose

n., the object toward which one strives or for which something exists; an aim or goal.

The other day… I was making grilled cheese sandwiches and I received a text from a friend. This friend said that they had just done something they hadn't done in a long time, which was to "pray." This person prayed for their friend who had a reoccurrence of cancer, and is not expected to live. The person's friend is a single parent of a child with disabilities, whose name begins with the letter "C."

Frankly, I was glad I was in the middle of making grilled cheese sandwiches because I truly needed to ponder. I am still pondering.

"I" want to "tell God," this is not right. This man and child who are struggling through life together should not be separated; to separate them would be unkind, unmerciful, and unloving…cruel. (I am not afraid to speak my truth.)

In fact, I think I may have told God exactly that, but in more "spiritually correct" lingo. It didn't seem to anger God…no lightning bolts flashed before or on me. But He did respond to me with the same directness that I approached him.

God is sovereign. He works everything "*according to the counsel of his will.*" He is the ultimate and limitless source of all power and authority over everything that exists…to the extent of being able to override all other powers and authorities…including disabilities, cancer, and death. Either I believe it, or I don't. I believe it. Even in my lack of understanding, I believe it.

I have been pondering a lot about God's will. The thing is, it seems God's will for me falls under his purpose for me, which is to bring Him glory. Maybe it is imperative I keep God's will for me within the bright light of his purpose for me. When I seem to focus in only on his will…the bright light of his purpose darkens, and I begin to flounder.

Glorifying God can be done with human disabilities of every kind. I have seen it through my friend's Down Syndrome sister who loved God ever joyously and always unquestionably.

Christ showed us that glorifying God can also be done in death and resurrection. While our bodies will not resurrect on the earth as we know it…the bodies of Believer's will definitely resurrect one day to the eternal heavenliness with God.

I will, and have prayed for this man's healing, for peace and endurance during his suffering and struggle, for placement for his son in a loving environment that cares for him as God created him, but mostly, I pray for the acceptance of God's perfect purpose to be accomplished in their lives…in God's divine way.

Within minutes of finalizing this ponder… I received word that the father had passed.

I shall ponder, and I shall definitely pray, for the son, whose name begins with the letter "C" with tears…

Appraisal

n., an act of assessing something or someone.

Our loan has been approved, inspections have been passed, measurements have been taken and disclosures have been disclosed. The final step in the purchase of our, new to us, home…is the appraisal.

Appraisals always seem to be the nail-biting thing. It seems to be particularly so in the current housing market because appraisals have come in extra low due to the expected downturn in the market as COVID mortgage forgiveness comes due at the end of the month.

Of course, this brings my ponder to; What will God's final appraisal of me be? What will the final judgement be like?

Quite heavy…no plans to stay with this ponder too long.

I have heard the analogy that all of our sanctifying schoolwork will be set before us…grades will be displayed on each paper. The book of life will be opened. In it is found the names of all believers. If our name is found in that book…a match stick from the cross of Jesus will be found behind our name, and our unpassing grades will be set ablaze. Believers will be granted entrance into the eternal heavenlies.

But what about our appraisals of others? The act of assessing someone or something from our own perspective. Putting our own grade on someone's sanctifying schoolwork.

Jesus doesn't tell me not to judge others…in fact, he desires for me to help others as they walk through the process of taking specks out of their own eye. But I am thinking I need to take serious caution because any actual, self-perceiving grade I put on someone else's sanctifying schoolwork will be kept until that final judgment day, and likely a photocopy of its correct or incorrectness will be added into my own grade book. Not something I want to see…even if it is ultimately set ablaze.

I shall put my red pen away…
and ponder…

Hope

～～～～～～～～～～～～～～～～～

v., to cherish a desire with anticipation; to want something to happen or be true.

The appraisal for our new house came back right where it needed to be. We are moving another step forward toward our new home…hopefully before the Fourth of July.

We put our house up for sale February 18, several weeks before the quarantine began. Elise and I both had hopes of hosting her original mid-May baby shower there.

In Psalm 42, there is this verse: "*Why are you cast down, O my soul, and why are you disquieted within me? Hope in God!*" It seems hope, when challenged, does not come easily for man.

Could it be that I am expressing a "desired outcome of uncertainty" vs. "a solid expectation of hope"…a biblical hope that comes as an off-shoot of God's will, His promises, His character?

Being clear on the Lord's promises and character is clearly documented in the Bible. I want to say His will is not, but I am challenged with my recent ponderings on God's will that it involves mercy, sacrifice, holiness, nonconformation, and transformation. It was rather clear.

In the end… Elise's desire/hope for a baby shower was challenged, and did come to pass in a rather delightful and unique way. My desire/hope for a new home was challenged, and did come to pass…even if it was in a rather undelightful way.

Yes, my hope may be challenged, but I must hold onto it with solid expectation.

I shall ponder…

Independence

n., not requiring or relying on something else.

Today is the day we celebrate American Independence (and the final approval of the wording of the Declaration of Independence).

I have always loved celebrating the Fourth of July. Until age seven, I lived in a town that was known for its Fourth of July Parade. My dad served in the navy and we were a family thankful for the meaning of the red, white, and blue.

I married a patriotic man, whose patriotism takes him further than a parade, hot dogs, and fireworks. He takes the wording of the Declaration of Independence and Constitution to heart.

The Declaration of Independence begins with what I think is one of the greatest sentences ever written…

"We hold these truths to be self-evident, that all men are created equal, that they are endowed by their Creator with certain unalienable Rights, that among these are Life, Liberty and the pursuit of Happiness."

All men are created equal.

Life

Liberty

The pursuit of happiness

It seems here in America we are still working on each of these "unalienable" rights. We are still working to overcome various kinds of racial, gender, and economic injustices. It seems we are still trying to decide when life begins. There still seems to be great tension between personal liberties and order. Most certainly…happiness has become something we feel entitled to…instead of something we are to pursue.

The thing is, America is a country that has never wavered on freedom of speech. Maybe we should use that right with an intention to communicate with humble dialogue…instead of overpowering, prideful commands. Just wondering.

Change starts with me, so I shall ponder…

Identity

n., to indicate who or what (someone or something) is.

Barry and I were on our morning circle of the RV park, puppies in tow, when I spotted an old truck in an overflow parking lot. I veered off our path to get a better look at the truck about one hundred feet away.

I was excited because I thought it was a Studebaker. Barry's first call was a Ford. We soon called out a Chevy. As we got closer and closer...we kept switching what make we thought the vehicle was. When we finally arrived, we learned that it was "none of the above" but a GMC. Well then, almost a Chevy.

It is easy to think we know something at first glance...by its headlights, the front grate, contour of lines, but it is not until we get up close and see its name...that we can claim its identity.

My name is Sandi, but at the "grate" of my being is a name identifying me as a "Child of the King." I am defined by how God contours my life...the destiny he appoints those wheels to take...the people he chooses for me to share cupholders with, and those who choose to come close enough to see "who I really am." Those who see that my identity is to make known Christ's identity.

On any given day...a "conversion" of my true identity can emerge. You know...trying to recontour who I am to fit in with the changing whims of society. Wheels that are grossly larger than need be...just in case I need to barrel over a log on the way to the grocery store. Or maybe overcompensating suspension lifts that require a ladder or elevator to gain entrance to the vehicle. Why do we do this to ourselves? What are we overcompensating for?

I am hardwired to gain my identity vertically through God. As I make "conversions" to who God made me... I begin a normal human struggle to look for my identity horizontally, in society. When I look in a mirror... I forget who I truly am.

Oddly, like this GMC truck, I find myself sitting in a parking lot...an "in-between" point. Not settled into a new church...a new ministry…not quite a grandma yet…not even a homeowner yet. But those things do not identify me… Christ does.

I shall ponder…

Laundry

~~~~~~

n., soiled clothes or linens that need to be washed.

I am heading over to Elise's apartment to help her with laundry. It seems in-utero Liberty is already getting in the way of her mama's ability to get the task done.

In our society, we often gauge the value of work based on compensation, title, and even the name of the place we work at. If you don't get paid, have a formal title, spend too much time in meetings, then we clearly are not at work.

But the truth about work is, it is far more about who we reflect when we work, than the finer details of our labor. God created work…he created man to work…to meet the needs of his creation and for his glory. Likely, that work will continue on the other side of heaven.

My daughter is officially on maternity leave. For all the moms out there… I say…her destined work, best work, most difficult work, most God-glorifying work is about to begin, and in several weeks, the fruit of true "labor" will be born.

Instead of overflowing email, will be overflowing laundry. Instead of organizing work tasks, will be organizing closet space. Instead of daily meetings with clients, will be nightly meetings with a hungry baby. Instead of going to a supervisor when she needs help, she will call her mom, and I am honored to help…

So instead of pondering… I am offering to do some laundry.

Space

n., the three-dimensional expanse in which all material objects are located.

Barry and I realized that the amount of space we have been living in…is less than the smallest bedroom in our new home. All of us are ready for more space.

I guess the Israelites traveled and housed entire families in portable tents…back in the day, *but* they did not have to rally for electrical outlets. We seem to have more techno "stuff" that needs charging than we have outlets in the RV. After many tedious months of trying… I am finally learning to share. But I'm over it.

Space is an unimaginable thing. We are limited to understanding its vastness by what we are able to see or creatively capture in our minds.

As creative as we humans are…our creative powers are very limited. We cannot create matter out of nothing; we simply can reorder it. If all the physicists, scientists and smartphones in the world were gathered together…a grain of sand could not be made. That small grain to which the Lord calls me to rest my faith.

God, on the other hand, by the mere words, *"Let there be,"* created the entire universe out of nothing…physicists, scientists, smartphones…even a "big bang," not needed.

On Christmas Eve 1968, in the most watched television broadcast at the time, Bill Anders, Jim Lovell, and Frank Borman, of Apollo 8 each read a passage from Genesis 1:1–10. They were the first humans to travel to the moon.

As big as the creation is, the Bible shows us that our Creator is even bigger. He is a powerful and omnipresent Creator. But He is also a loving, compassionate Father who cares for all man, especially the vulnerable, poor, and needy.

God also loves the weak and messed-up sinner like me, sending His one and only Son to this tiny speck in the universe called earth,

so that when I believed in Him, I might have eternal life with Him...
in glory.

Looking forward to more electrical outlets and space, but
pondering the big, powerful, omnipresent, loving, compassionate
Creator...who cares desperately for me.

I shall ponder...

Church

~~~~~~

n., a people and place of worship.

Today we are going to attend what will likely become our new church home. It is attended by our daughter and son-in-law and his family. They have attended this church through Brad's entire childhood. That says something to me about both the leadership of the church and the commitment level of Brad's family.

Churches are messy. They are filled with people like me. I can relate to these people. They are also filled with people unlike me. This requires a little more work, and as an "outspoken introvert," I'd rather sit in my same spot, at the same church service time, and make a quick exit to the car immediately following service. I have progressed, but not conquered my social inabilities.

Churches are meant to be filled with people of every color and age. They are meant to be filled with both the spiritually mature, the new convert, the nonbeliever and everything in between. They are meant to be filled with both those who read the Bible and pray, and those who do not. Those who struggle with addictions and those who do not. Friends who utter unnecessary, harsh words and friends who walk with you…carrying your cross…through a most difficult time.

Churches are meant to be filled with those whom God loves… man.

God has many plans for his church…one is to make his grace known to the world. He seems to be choosing not to do that with a bunch of perfect people, living together in perfect harmony, but with "unique," differently "gifted," differently "challenged," "sinful" humans like me.

I suppose my ponder comes from a conviction that I am called to "get to know" these people, who "all" are actually quite like me, so that I can share grace back and forth with them.

I shall ponder…

Heat

n., a form of energy produced by the motion of molecules.

Yesterday, we were blessed with a surprise lunch visit from Elise and Brad. However, the barbecue broke. Five people (and two dogs) in a small RV…while prepared barbecue pork cooked in the cast iron skillet…in 103+ temperature…is not ideal. The poor AC in the RV just couldn't keep up.

Barry made a pool reservation for Elise and I to go swimming after lunch. The water was *perfect.* Not so cold that you spend the reserved hour trying to get your entire body submerged, but cool enough that it is still refreshing once you do.

Brad and Barry made a run to a market down the street known for its great ice cream sandwiches and met us at the pool. Cool bodies, double thick ice cream sandwiches marked a moment of pure refreshment.

There is a verse in Isaiah: *"And there shall be a tabernacle for a shadow in the daytime from the heat, and for a place of refuge, and for a covert from storm and from rain"* (Isa. 18:4).

In a thought, yesterday's refreshment could be placed with a cool pool and yummy ice cream sandwich, but both were temporary. It is the tabernacle, the meeting place between God and I that provides me the true and lasting shadow of refuge.

The thing is, while the tabernacle is God's meeting place with man; it is also a place of sacrifice.

The ultimate sacrifice for man's sin has been placed, but for man, for me, hardship will still come. The heat of hardship drives me deeper into the all-sufficient, refreshing grace of God.

When heat comes, I shall thirst, not for a temporary ice cream sandwich, but for the security and strength of an all-sufficient God.

Today, I again will visit the refreshment of the pool, and God's grace.

And I shall ponder…

Growth

~~~~~~

n., full development; maturity.

We move into our new home this weekend.... I have once again secured the living room as my "art studio" and laid claim to the backyard as my garden.

The backyard is a mess, which excites me, offering a blank slate to let my garden skills work freely. My first plans are for raised vegetable beds offering us vegetables of plenty, which is hysterical because I currently have tomato, cucumber, and zucchini plants in pots outside the RV, which are wilting with inattention.

I am not sure why this happened. I suppose a good portion has to do with habit, location, and a secured watering system. Whatever the case, I am reminded that what a gardener does or doesn't do matters.

The thing is, as a gardener I can plant seeds in a conducive plot of land with the best sunlight and soil... I can tend, water, and weed the garden, but I have no control over which seeds will grow into a plant. God must cause that growth. God's sovereignty knows how things will turn out long before they ever happen. His sovereignty also calls me to work...such as to tend my garden...my spiritual garden.

I suppose tending the garden of the soul begins with providing a conducive environment for growth...prayer, confession, spiritual food, hope, but in the end... I have no idea what growth will actually happen.

Case in point... We have been living in our RV for the past seven weeks. It seemed obvious the Lord was going to grow me some "patience." Admittedly, patience did not grow, but what did grow was my ability to "offer grace" to others who were just as impatient and tired of living in a space smaller than our new master bathroom as me.

I did not have control over what was going to "grow" in me, but was able to offer enough of a "conducive environment" for "something" to grow in me...even if it wasn't what I expected.

I am excited to tend to both of my gardens... I shall toil, pray, hope, and ponder...

Fence

n., a barrier or other upright structure enclosing an area of ground to mark a boundary, control access, or prevent escape.

We now live on a corner lot and are extending our back side yard by moving our fence out toward the sidewalk. Our motor home is set to rest there.

Having lived under the protection of gated communities the last fifteen years… I am thankful for the tight "hedge of protection" our fence and cement guy is providing for our new home.

This took me to ponder the "hedge of protection." The idea generally comes from the book of Job…it makes sense…the poor guy certainly needed a hedge of protection! But what I was unsure of was the situation surrounding the hedge. Did God build the hedge or did he call Job to build the hedge? Does scripture specifically call out the hedge for protection against the evil one? Why does Job's hedge seem rather faulty? It wasn't long before I realized I used this term frequently, prayerfully, and it seems…rather (scripturally) loosely.

Hmmmm….

It turns out "hedge of protection" does not appear in scripture in those exact words, or even in the context with which I was using it. In Job 1:10 and 11, Satan claims that if God removes the "hedge," the blessings of prosperity He has provided, Job will curse Him.

God does remove the hedge. Job does lose almost everything that prospered him. Job does *not* curse God. In fact, Scripture tells us that he fell to the ground…worshipped and said: "*The Lord has given and the Lord has taken away. Blessed be the name of the Lord*" *(Job 1:21).*

The thing is, this context is not about the "hedge," but the response to the hedge. It is about worshipping the Lord whether He gives or takes away.

There are many scriptures that speak of God's protection over His people. I picture spiritual airbags for when I crash and spiritual motion detectors, alarms and pepper spray that defuses danger when it is near.

The truth is, I need protection because I am vulnerable, because I live in a "fallen" world. In some instances, the spiritual air bags may not deploy…the pepper spray may not diffuse danger. My only absolute, ultimate protection and security…is faith in my sovereign Lord.

In Psalm 91, God does not promise that the worst this world has to offer won't come upon us, but when it does, we are not alone, abandoned, or destroyed.

The Theology of Sandi now believes my protection is not in a "hedge," but is in my faith, in the sovereignty of our Father.

I shall ponder…

Waterpik

n., portable electric appliance that uses a stream of water under force to remove food particles from between the teeth and to massage the gums.

Last year, after the long and expensive process of a dental implant… I finally invested in a Water Pick. At the time, Barry never quite got on board, but found it humorous when I inadvertently sprayed either myself, the mirror, or random surrounding objects with the shooting water.

Yesterday, I finally unpacked the box with my Pik and set it up for immediate use. Our new environment enticed Barry to get on board the Water Pick train. After I gave him a quick overview of how the thing worked…there was immediate inadvertent spraying of himself, the mirror, and surrounding objects…all in one blast. Yes, I found it rather humorous!

The thing about a Water Pik is, it is not meant to replace brushing your teeth, but to remove "leftovers" in-between the teeth…that can turn into bacteria…that can harden into plaque…that can turn into cavities…that can turn into gum disease…that can turn into expensive dental bills.

Just wondering what lingering, "leftover" emotions I am holding on to that can turn into spiritual bacteria, that can harden, create cavities and disease in my heart.

Resentment comes to mind.

Being the verbally forthright person that I am…resentment doesn't seem to build up when my tongue is free and totally unleashed.

The tricky thing is: when I walk holding the Spirit's fruit close to my heart…some "leashing" is required to maintain my words in love.

The problem is: sometimes it is just easier to "not say anything at all," than to figure out how to speak truth "nicely." (Thank you, Thumper!) In steps resentment.

I suppose the solution is to take a mere two minutes to Water Pik with prayer...to ask for the right words to speak truth in love. Simple, yes, but like flossing, it often is just "easier" not to do it... especially daily.

Glad to have "unleashed" my Water Pik from its storage box... challenging myself to take those ever so precious two minutes to pray over speaking my truth nicely...

Pondering...

Lizard

~~~~~~

n., a reptile with movable eyelids, ears that are outside the body, and has two to four legs.

Shivers are running down my spine just writing the definition. I am not a reptile person.

My daughter and son in law had a two-legged slithering lizard in their apartment. I wasn't there, but caught the excitement in real-time postings (and gladly from afar) on the Marco Polo app.

I "binged" how to both find and catch a lizard... I helped (gladly from afar).

I used to watch our dog Franklyn unsuccessfully try to catch the lizards in our Rio Vista backyard. It was entertaining (gladly from afar).

Reptiles have always creeped me out, but I justified my disgust after reading a book by C. S. Lewis titled The Great Divorce. In the book, a Ghost who has been kept out of heaven tries to keep his pet sin, a red lizard. The Ghost is constantly found rebuking the lizard that lives on his shoulder. An angel arrives and asks him if he would like for the lizard to be silenced. The Ghost is anxious for the lizard to be silenced until he realizes the means of silencing is death, then he begins to negotiate a better way to silence the lizard...in a more gradual way. The lizard whispers his own negotiations into the Ghost's ear...promises the Ghost knows can't be kept, but are far more comforting...

The thing is, sin is best slayed, not trained. I've tried it.... am still trying it...

My "binged" research told me that lizards like to hide in the dark...a flash of light most often will cause them to move...creating opportunity to remove its presence.

I like my sin to be hidden in the dark. Not just so others can't see it, but so I can deny it's there. When that flash of "light" comes... it is my opportunity to remove its presence...

I shall ponder...

Family

n., a primary social group consisting of parents and their offspring, the principal function of which is provision for its members.

We have excitedly and exhaustingly…moved into our new home. "Moved in" being defined as: packed boxes that are intermingled with possessions that have already found their new place within our home, and a two-car garage that can "almost" hold one car.

This move was quite different than others…we moved in the sweltering summer instead of the usual Christmas season, the necessity for COVID masks and gloves, we are old, but the most significant difference was having a son-in-law (and his dad) who worked tirelessly for two days moving boxes, plants, and "stuff" from a storage unit to our new home. I really like having a son-in-law.

What I appreciate most is not that he worked hard in the heat, but the commitment, affection, and honor he shows his pregnant wife, and her family.

We desire for our new home to be filled with family.

The thing is, while we are moving closer to one family group, which brings joy…we are also moving farther away from another, which brings sadness. Our statistically horrifying, seven moves have taught me that…familiarity…comfort…longevity…space…does not create a home, but family does…weather near or far.

Barry and I want our home to be purposeful. We want those who enter to feel like family. We want the "aroma" of respect, laughter, love, and the Spirit's fruit. We want the aroma of Christ.

While the pandemic will keep our east coast, midwest and Cali "families" from entering our new home…we will be intentional with the time we have to focus on the four generations of Liberty's family that can be present. We will also be intentional to create virtual time with those who can't, and the sweet aroma of "all family" will be present when Liberty enters this home.

I shall ponder…

Suggestion and Compromise

Suggestion: *n.*, an idea, plan, or action that is offered for acceptance or rejection.

Compromise: *n.*, the settlement of a dispute by concessions on both or all sides.

We've had a lot of "projects" making this house our home. When I am project manager of a task, Barry has this recurrent phrase he uses: "Can I make a suggestion?"

While in my "I am determined to make this work the way I first envisioned" mode...the answer is likely "no." The suggestion comes anyway. The suggestion is "rejected"; the suggestion is repeated because it wasn't really offered with the option of rejection.... A stall happens...

When I am taking a more open-minded approach to my role as project manager...things go quite differently...more smoothly. The suggestions still come...still may or may not be accepted, but I have learned that compromise is a great tool for moving forward.

The Bible councils that compromise is needed when dealing with the complexities and ambiguities of sinful man, but not acceptable when dealing with a holy and omnipotent God.

Oddly, it took me a while to figure this out. I mean...if I can compromise on a suggestion of how art is displayed in our home... shouldn't I be allowed to expect God to compromise with me about how my "attitude" is displayed to said "suggestor?" Yeah, no!

The Theology of Sandi believes that compromise with man is a medication to help heal...however, compromise with God is a drug used dangerously and without prescription.

My attitude is the area I am most likely to try a justification or compromise process with God. It usually starts with the words "I deserve." Then I remember Christ...who came to stand in my place mercifully for what I truly deserve. If I allow myself to stall for a ponder... I am able to let go of my self-justification. The question is, "Will I?"

I shall ponder...

Frustration

n., a deep chronic sense or state of insecurity and dissatisfaction arising from unresolved problems or unfulfilled needs.

I let frustration overtake me the other day. No big happenings… just a consistent bunching of little things that kept adding up…

I dropped my "Grandma Sandi" Yeti, filled with diet coke, twice (No! *Not* the Grandma Sandi Yeti!). I mis-communicated with others more than twice. While watering the plants in the front yard, my legs became instantly covered with ants. Dog sees cat on the other side of the screen…dog runs through screen to catch said cat…it is the dog that is hard to catch. The pieced square I was working on for a "cousin quilt" came out hideously "wavy," a good pressing did not cure the problem, that was just the beginning of my morning…

Frustration or self-pity? Let me ponder…

Frustration comes when I stumble into the proverbial mud pit. Self-pity is when I decide to swim around in the mud pit for more drama and sympathy instead of working my way out.

I am happy to report, in this instance, I did not wallow around in the mud pit of self-pity too long. But it did take some real "work" to get myself out. I prayed…asked God to guide me out…assumed (I called it "had faith") he would snatch me right out of that pit. However, comma, God rarely takes me directly from A to B. It is usually more like A to Z.

It seems… God's purpose for me is not speed, but sanctification. Hmmmm.

Paul speaks of plans he had in his letters to various churches. He told the Philippian Church that he was going to travel from Jerusalem to Spain. However, while passing through Rome he found himself in prison. Now *that* is a mud pit. Paul never lost faith…never lost his focus on the Lord.

The thing is, am I focusing on God, or the mud?

Sometimes God's purpose for us is to do work in that mud pit. Sometimes it changes us. Sometimes it changes the world.

I shall ponder…

Fried Green Tomatoes

n., unripe tomatoes, sliced, dipped in egg and cornmeal or flour, and fried.

The lightning and thunder pulled me out of a peaceful prayer time this morning. The lightning was bright and the thunder came immediately. I was *not* all about it! I hesitantly peeked out our bedroom sliding glass door and saw that my potted tomato plant had fallen over. Fried green tomatoes?

According to the Urban Dictionary…the definition for Fried Green Tomatoes is: to take someone's parking spot in a rude fashion. Who knew?

A few moments later…a huge wind storm with rain turned the sky gray, blowing dust, branches and almost all the planks from our older side fence into the air. Auntie Em, Uncle Henry…!

I am brought to scripture…

> *For as the lightning flashes and lights up the sky from one side to the other, so will the Son of Man be in his day.* (Luke 17:24 and Matt. 24:7)

> *So Christ, having been offered once to bear the sins of many, will appear a second time, not to deal with sin but to save those who are eagerly waiting for him.* (Heb. 9:28)

> *Then we who are alive, who are left, will be caught up together with them in the clouds to meet the Lord in the air, and so we will always be with the Lord.* (1 Thess. 4:17)

There is, however, another part to this scriptural truth.

For then there will be great tribulation, such as has not been from the beginning of the world until now, no, and never will be. (Matt. 24:21)

Immediately after the tribulation of those days the sun will be darkened, and the moon will not give its light, and the stars will fall from heaven, and the powers of the heavens will be shaken. (Matt. 24:29)

I believe Jesus is coming back again one day...at a time no one knows...on the clouds of heaven with power and great glory.

I believe the Lord will snatch me and all my fellow Believers up to live with Him in holy eternity.

I believe there will be a time of tribulation and affliction and also a time for the accomplishment of God's redemption.

I believe that all Scripture is given by the inspiration of God, and is profitable for doctrine, for reproof, for correction, for instruction in righteousness.

I believe...

What do you believe?

Time to ponder...

Evacuation

n., the clearance of personnel, animals, or materiel from a given locality.

It was a telephone call that pulled me out of a peaceful prayer time. My daughter was calling to warn us that the evacuation line for the Napa/Sonoma fire (also called LNU fire) was literally a mile from our home. I peered out the sliding glass door and saw a thick blanket of smoke overhead. I opened the door to take a photo of the bright, red sun outside and the reality of heat vs. smoke was startling.

We knew the right thing to do, but we prayed anyway. A peace, a calmness enveloped me that reminded me why I should pray even when I "*do*" know the right thing to do.

We were scheduled to leave in a week for a road trip to attend one of my "inner circle" friend's wedding in Iowa, so we packed the RV as if we weren't coming home until after the road trip. I'm not gonna lie…there were definite moments when the calmness left me…. I'm sure we'll laugh about them later.

I always wondered about the decision-making process of what to take along in such a situation. My process was to step back and pray. I wanted to ponder…but there was no time. Could I live without this stuff? I desperately wanted to throw my sewing machines and some of the art on our walls in the RV but knew it wasn't realistic. So I grabbed my phone and began taking a video of our possessions room by room…a surreal moment.

Once exhausted and packed up in the RV, we headed out. We had not discussed with each other where "out" was going to be. Our daughter called to let us know they were evacuating also and heading south for cleaner air. She asked us where we were heading. "McDonald's," we said.

After loading up on burgers, fries, and drinks we headed toward Highway 5. I can't explain the oddity of driving "somewhere" without having a destination plan. The fire was coming from the north-west and heading east, so we eventually decided south seemed like a good plan.

While on southbound Highway 5, we received the "official orders" to evacuate. The fire had jumped the highway and was headed for the hills directly behind our house. Reality set in. We may not have a home to go back to. It's that moment when I remember how many times I have claimed God as Sovereign. I take a pause...a ponder, and claim God, still sovereign, but it means more to me now.

We settled in Coalinga for our first night's stop. We have not seen blue sky since we left and we all have non-COVID headaches and sore throats. Life gets better when we eat the salad and fruit that had been smashed tightly into the fridge for dinner.

Quickly, our hearts take a downturn when we plug into our hotspot and view some of the news broadcasts. Soon, the Holy Spirit peace begins to leave...pressure, tension, tightness, and acid reflux takes its place. We determine "news" cannot change anything in our plight and shut down the hot spot. Barry plays computer games and I read. We soon fall into a peaceful sleep... Nighty night.

Tomorrow I shall ponder...

Cauliflower

n., a variety of cabbage (*Brassica oleraceavar botrytis*) having a dense white mass of fleshy flower stalks that form the head.

I mentioned in my last post that my decision-making process during our evacuation was quite "surreal." While videoing those things that meant a lot to me, I went to this place…that was the most unemotional, rational place I had ever worked from. That place where speed was an option.

For some reason…that place left me when we got to the refrigerator. It makes no sense. We had just purchased a Costco membership with Brad and Elise and had our fridge crispers full of large bags holding vegetables of different types.

I was able to decide not to evacuate my sewing machines that are worth thousands of dollars, but could not decide which veggies to cram into our much smaller RV fridge. I started losing it when I saw Barry had decided to throw away the cauliflower; it's funny now…. I think….

In retrospect, the cauliflower decision wasn't really about keeping vs. wasting cauliflower, but was really about coming to a somewhat subconscious resolve that the cauliflower presented an opportunity to release some of my pent-up anxiety through unloving and unnecessary words spewed at my husband.

Decisions can be both easy and difficult…simple and complex…necessary and unnecessary. Deciding the fate of the cauliflower was clearly easy and difficult. Deciding where we were going to evacuate to…was both simple and complex with COVID, fires and heat all around us. Deciding to release pent up anxiety was necessary… deciding to release it on my husband was not.

The thing is, as a Christ follower…if I ask God to guide me… He will. His first step of guidance is through scripture. If I get "off track" He will correct and guide me back onto His path…it is called repentance and forgiveness.

After a good ponder…the "Theology of Sandi" has concluded that the Lord is not as concerned with my right or wrong decisions as he is if I am making them lovingly or not.

I shall ponder…

Plagues

n., a highly infectious, usually fatal, epidemic disease; a pestilence.

Barry and I had a short conversation about the craziness of 2020: the COVID pandemic, the lightning and fires, and the catastrophically large hurricanes. Barry made a comment: "The world needs to wake up and pay attention." That comment led me to a ponder, is God sending "plagues" to grab our attention? Is it the world that needs to pay attention, or Believers of Christ? Is this a sign of the End-Times? This required me to search scripture.

The "Theology of Sandi" is coming to realize that the "ten plagues" found in the book of Exodus are not so much about judgment as a call for repentance and God willing his power, supremacy and "Creator rights" over Israel, Egypt and all the earth.

Scripture reveals to us that God governs the following: *the wind, lightning, snow, frogs, gnats, flies, locusts, quail, worms, fish, sparrows, grass, plants, famine, the sun, prison doors, blindness, deafness, paralysis, fever, every disease, travel plans, the hearts of kings, nations, murderers, spiritual deadness,* and on and on.

God's ultimate goal is to uphold and display his glory. Scripture tells us it also happens to be for the enjoyment of His redeemed people. Maybe what plagues us most is our misplaced identity in Christ.

I shall ponder…

The End-Times

n., the time of the prophesied end of the world: *Armageddon*

"The End-Times" have come up in several conversation I have had with people as well. Is this craziness a sign of the end-times?… possibly, but does that mean the end is near in time as "we know it?" Scripture tells us we will not know the time, but it does record signs and wonders we will see.

The end-times will be preceded by the following:

- Great *earthquakes* and *tribulation* such as has not occurred since the beginning of the world until now, nor ever will.
- *Plagues* and *famines* in various places.
- *Terrors* and *great signs* from heaven.
- The *sun darkening,* the *moon not giving its light,* the *stars falling* from heaven, and the *powers* of the heavens being *shaken.*
- Days like those of *Noah.*
- *Wonders* in the sky and on earth and of *blood, fire, vapor, and smoke.*
- The *sun* shall be turned to darkness and the *moon* to blood.
- *Wars* and *rumors* of wars.
- Nation rising *against* nation, and kingdom *against* kingdom.
- Many *falling away, betraying,* and *hating* one another.
- *False prophets* will come in Christ's name, showing great signs and wonders, saying, "I am the Christ," and will mislead many, even the elect, if possible.
- God pouring out *his Spirit* on all flesh.

- The *Gospel being preached* in the whole world as a testimony to all the nations.
- *Prophecies, visions, and dreams.*

God's ultimate plan upon his return is that *"it shall come to pass that everyone who calls upon the name of the Lord shall be saved."*
I shall ponder...

Scripture Resources:
Exodus 7–12
Matthew 24
Luke 21
Acts 2
Joel 2
1 Timothy 4
2 Timothy 3
2 Thessalonians 2
Daniel 10 and 11
Revelation 11

Draft

n., a preliminary version of a piece of writing. A compulsory recruitment for military service. A current of cool air in a room or other confined space. Beer or other drink that is kept in and served from a barrel or tank rather than from a bottle or can.

Today is draft day for my Fantasy Football League. I have researched, prepped, and reenacted the information found in the "little black book" I left at home in the haste of packing. I have revisited my "Learning Fantasy Football" blog, practiced using the "mock draft" system on the ESPN APP (ended up with a fine team per my son-in-law). Most importantly, I will find a draft...a brewski...to "pop" when the process is through and I have my team..."Sandi's Tight Ends"!

I have said it too many times... I am an academic...the academics don't necessarily come to me easily, but I must keep working to understand, and once I understand... I keep working to achieve knowledge that is beyond what I need to know. When it comes to Fantasy Football, and especially Football in general...this academia clearly is going to be a life-long process. Though I am becoming more familiar with Fantasy Football...the game itself still completely eludes me!

In my research... I learned about a thing called "tanking." Tanking is when a team gives up a game, losing intentionally to acquire a better position in the draft. Who knew?

I "tanked" in FF unintentionally last year. Came in absolutely last and earned the "tank award." However, it turns out I don't get better positioning in today's draft. *What?!*

Sometimes the "sanctification process" feels like tanking. There have been seasons in my spiritual walk filled with spiritual victory, and seasons of repeated defeat. I'll be honest... I have boldly, bravely, asked my league manager, Christ, "What the heck? What are you thinking?" To my recollection I haven't asked that question in times of victory...interesting.

At times… I wonder if God is tanking me. Allowing me repeated defeat for an "ulterior motive." At those times… I head to the locker room, for some deep inner conversation. In that locker room… I am reminded sanctification is a team sport…we are to trust the process together, and as God's people we are "*to stir up one another to love and good works, not neglecting to meet together, as is the habit of some, but encouraging one another, and all the more as you see the Day drawing near*" (Heb. 10:24–25).

The truth is, God *does* allow defeat for a purpose. A sanctifying purpose. A holy purpose. But I must always remember our victory is in heaven…not in the things of this earth. Everyone who walks with the Lord experiences the same kind of process. Sometimes it's victory…sometimes it's defeat…sometimes it is the feeling of being tanked, but always…it's growing in the holiness of God…a process I can trust…we can trust, because "*the God of peace [will] himself sanctify [me] completely*" (1 Thess. 5:23).

So much to ponder…

Attention

n., to make someone notice you.

We are in Oklahoma and there was a cantankerous thunder and lightning storm above us early this morning. Still not a fan. I have pondered how God shows his strength and power through such storms. That power is unsurmountable. But in my continued ponderings... I also wonder if he is trying to grab my attention. This morning's thunderstorms certainly captured the attention of the three humans and two pups in our motor home.

The thing is, He captured our attention without words. We are all standing at attention, but are unable to interpret what it is He may be saying. If we all went to the Bible...we would all likely receive something different from God...a different passage...a different application to our life, and that's okay because sometimes God speaks personally, and sometimes he speaks corporately.

I am wondering if sometimes God just needs to capture my attention; to remind me he is out there. The question is will I pay attention? Once the cantankerous moment is gone, who or what do I continue to pay attention to?

God can powerfully grab my attention, but it becomes my choice what I do next. Will I awaken and head to scripture/prayer, or will I head to social media wondering what others are saying about the storm? What "voices" will I search out to have shaping power for my beliefs?

I believe God uses the voices of His people to have shaping power in my life. But when God makes the attempt to grab or fix my attention on Him through a lightning storm, a song, a circumstance... I need to be careful I am paying extended attention to Him.

In Mark 4:24, Jesus told his disciples the importance of paying close attention to *"what they hear"* that the attitude in which they receive the word of Jesus profoundly affects how much more they—we—will hear from Him.

Am I paying attention? Who and what am I paying attention to? Is it the Gospel and the other words of Scripture, or is it my "emotions of the moment," an emotional high that causes me to maybe do, say, experience, spend more than I should…or emotional low plagued by self-doubt and pity that causes me to do nothing at all?

Hmmmm… I shall pay attention…patiently…

And ponder…

Cantankerous

adj., ill-tempered, quarrelsome, difficult to handle.

Cantankerous Oklahoma lightning and thunderstorm #2...on steroids...hit us last night. Barry and I were out chasing down the sunset when the weather drastically and quickly took a turn toward darkness. Again...not a fan!

I was hanging out the window, shotgun, taking a photo of the Drummond Ranch (Pioneer Woman) mailboxes across from the entrance to their ranch. The wind, the rain, the thunder, the lightning, but ohhh, what a great photo op...that rusted yellow/orange mailbox against the coming storm...much more beautiful in person.

We headed back toward "our" RV ranch where my mom was "trying" to relax with the pups. Immediately above us was a *huge* lightning strike with an immediate bomb of thunder...pretty sure I peed my panties a little. Just ahead on the road was a small fire where the lightning had hit. Luckily, it was a wet...instead of dry...lightning storm. I was the only one that seemed concerned. The small fire was casually circled by "locals" who seemed to enjoy the sociality of the moment.

By the time we got back to our RV ranch, the monsoon of rain tempted me to sleep in the car...until more thunder and lightning struck. I left my camera in the car and ran to the RV with a broken umbrella which got quite tangled in my hair, but the run to safety was successful.

Snuggled into our bed, with Harriet our nervous dog, shaking in my lap, I asked the Lord, What is it that you want my constant attention for? What am I missing? The response did not come immediately, but the assuredness of His desire for me...his nonverbal words for me were real, and personal.

I will ponder his desire for me and his nonverbal words....

Another thunder and lightning storm is on the way...

Maybe I am the one who is "cantankerous"...

Again... I shall ponder....

Creation Perfectus

Creation: n., a basic Christian belief that God created all things, and that all three persons of the godhead were involved in the act. God spoke, and by the power of his creative word, it happened (Gen. 1:1–3; Job 33:4; Ps. 33:6, 9, 102:25; John 1:1–3; Heb. 1:1–2). *Perfectus: adj.*, perfect, finished, complete.

I just began a Bible study in Genesis. After completing the first week of study, the ponder that kept coming to mind was "God's Glory." I challenged myself to contrive my best attempt at a definition. After a bit of pondering and study this is what I "imperfectly" came up with...

God's glory is the fullness of all He is. The sum of which includes His omniscient wisdom, omnipotent power and all-encompassing omnipresence...the culmination of which sets Him apart from all man, and his holiness.

My weeks' study in Genesis 1, took me to a ponder on the aspect of God's glory through creation. My ponder turned into a daydream of the mountains with their many gray, blue, and white hues, uncountable shades of green and brown, a nearby valley with wildflowers flickering in the wind on a warm, yet breezy spring day and of course, the ever-present babbling brook. "Creation Perfectus."

However, comma, God's glory in creation is not done well by way of a daydream. I must go further. Our recent fire evacuation and extreme weather road trip taught me the importance of trying to view the larger picture...more than what I see before me on my personal canvas.

God's glory is revealed in the beautiful and also the powerful; thunder, lightning, fire, and unexpected and unseasonal blizzard storms in Wyoming.

God's glory is beyond my perception of "Creation Perfectus" and includes God's display of supremacy over all the earth requiring me to reconsider my perception of perfection. God's glory is not just in the grandeur of his power but also his unadorned, peaceful presence. That presence I embrace and sometimes reject when I cry out to him in my suffering.

The Bible tells me God's glory is also revealed in me. As "Creation In-perfectus" as I may be, I am still His image bearer. Sometimes I make brush strokes on my "life-canvas" God does not desire. Those strokes I know are not intended for my canvas, but I determine to add them anyway. However, there are also those strokes that He did intend…a variety of strokes that depict His character and also stronger, darker strokes such as suffering, repentance, and redemption.

What strokes am I going to apply to my canvas today?

I shall ponder…

Pand-ark-mic

My Bible study took me to Genesis 8 this morning. I took the time to do the math and realized Noah and the fam were on that ark much longer than I realized. I knew it was longer than forty days and forty nights, but I didn't realize it was actually an entire year (plus five days).

I am thinking we can all relate with Noah to some degree during this pandemic. It seems like families are shut in to their own ark…floating about waiting for the COVID flood to end. Some of us "unmask" the doors to our ark upon first realization that the rain has stopped…others wait a little more patiently for a sign the waters are receding, and still others are waiting for the COVID waters to completely recede allowing dry, "safe" land to be proven.

God told Noah there was going to be a forty-day flood… He did not tell Noah he was going to be quarantined inside the arc for just over a year. As the thirty-day increments pressed on and on… Noah displayed his patience. I suppose it helped not having a smart-phone with apps professing upcoming weather conditions or a news channel/website "spinning" information in the direction he saw fit.

God has ushered some to the other side of heaven during this COVID flood. He will usher most to the other side of the pandemic. When we arrive there…it is not the one with the most toilet paper or Clorox wipes that proves himself "wisest" or "righteous," but the one who takes the time to build an altar to the Lord. The one who acknowledges God's sovereignty. The one who chose to be obedient to God's unique plan for their lives. The one who builds a holy place on which to worship the Lord.

On the other side of the pandemic… I hope I am not most concerned with who did it "right" or "wrong" but how God "grew me" through it. I hope I live knowing my days are numbered. That life is short and eternity is long. I hope I release some of the trivialities of my life to make way for those things I learned are most important…relationships, ministry, Holy Spirit guided opportunities and my walk with God.

I shall ponder…

Little Things

Matters or issues that are or seem to be of minor significance.

Our furniture finally arrived yesterday…what was first targeted as three weeks…turned into three months plus three weeks. I am normally a patient person, but I learned when I am not… I am *not*!

Anyway, before I digress too far, this isn't my pondering of long-awaited furniture. It is my pondering of the little things.

The new family room furniture allowed my prayer chair to be delivered back to its spot in our bedroom. Ahhhhhhh… I could hardly wait to rest myself within its boundaries!

This morning, while waiting for my coffee to brew… I high-tailed it back to the bedroom and placed the electric blanket over my prayer chair. The long-awaited crisp, fall weather allowed me to turn that baby to "almost" high. As I returned to retrieve my freshly brewed coffee, I was anxious to maneuver off the "adult proof" power sealed, tiny piece of aluminum that kept me from the first taste of my long-awaited favorite holiday creamer.

My prayer chair…darkness…silence…crisp fall weather…coffee with my favorite holiday creamer…time with the Lord… I was giddy with delight.

I took time to thank the Lord for each of those things. For Himself…a human being without sin who died on the cross for me. For a prayer chair that looks simply like a chair to everyone else but to me holds history of my prayers, studies, ponderings, and meetings with the Lord. For darkness and crisp fall weather that rotates without fail. For silence that is desperately hard to find. For the feeling of anticipation and joy as I take the first sip of morning coffee.

The little things…the things easily taken for granted…

I must ponder God's perspective. How much do the "little things" in my life bring joy and delight to the Lord…turning a smirk into a smile…choosing to cover an attitude with love or choosing peace over anxiety…having an attitude of patience when things don't go "my" way (even when furniture target delivery dates are continuously pushed out and the sales associate at the store is rude) or patience while my husband "fills his tank" with conversation from peeps he meets "along the way" while I am desperately trying to fill mine with silence...creating "history" that glorifies Him in my prayer chair and in my daily walk with him?

Hmmmmm... I must ponder....

Compromise

n., a settlement of differences in which each side makes concessions.

I am now studying in Genesis 19; scripture turns from Abraham toward his brother, Lot, who has chosen to reside in Sodom. A study on Lot's life weaved me to realize the "steady progression of compromise" in his life.

Lot went from looking toward Sodom (Gen. 13), to pitching his tent toward Sodom (Gen. 13:12), to living in Sodom and losing everything when Sodom was attacked (Gen. 14), to standing at the gate of Sodom, indicating he was now a leader in town (Gen. 19).

What struck me wasn't that he ended up in such a compromised situation, but how he gradually declined to it. It seems it all started with his gazing "toward Sodom."

It immediately struck me how compromise in my own life generally doesn't happen swiftly, but as a gradual decline. I prayed, "Lord, what am I *looking toward*? What am I gazing at that can be or is the catalyst to spiritual compromise in my life?"

I will be honest…what first came to mind was the "gazing" I had overcome. I no longer gaze toward houses I longingly wish I could inhabit, or more importantly…back toward a house I wish I still inhabited.

Next up, I realized how I longingly desire for a trim/thin body however, I also longingly gaze at cookies, bread, extra portions at meal time and of course, potato chips. This realization taught me the danger of gazing "toward" such pleasures, but a step deeper is when I start partaking…by figuratively pitching my tent in the pantry.

At first, I didn't realize I was going deeper within my soul when I thought of my longing for a truck. Simple right? I have always been a truck girl. I still long for one. But as I laughed at the seemingly unimportance of it all… I felt a tug that there was something deeper for me to realize.

The thing is, trucks are meant to transport stuff…not gather it. I have gathered stuff along the way that was meant to be transported to the dump, but I jammed it out of sight into baggage... never meant to be carried...taking up space and adding weight as I travel along the way. Stuff like anger, resentment, fear, frustration, and most heavy...regret.

I ask myself...where does the compromise of transport vs. gather begin? For me...it begins as I gaze forward at issues that belong to others or is simply trash on the side of the road. It travels deeper as I co-dependently pick up and carry "baggage" I was never meant to carry...it eventually becomes a part of me as I pitch a tent for it to rest in the back of my truck, and I stand at its gate professing there is no more space for God's intended purposes... I am full and overwhelmed.

However, comma, this is not the end. God rescues the righteous. He teaches us. He provides for us... He warns us to not "look back" at what he has destroyed, but forward to the wondrous work He is creating.

Am I gazing...each moment...in the right direction?

I shall ponder...

Godspeed

n., a prosperous journey.

This morning when Barry and Franklyn left for "work" (early morning errands and diet Cokes from McDonald's), he texted me a quick photo of a brilliant presunrise. I begged him to come back and pick me up, which he did. I jumped quickly into the car with my bare feet, bedhead hair, jammies, and camera…

It was so refreshing, so "right" to be chasing a sunrise. It was a game for Barry to find the best spot, with the best view before the sunrise quickly faded away into sunlight.

In the midst of all the movement… I was able to sit in a form of stillness, and ponder. My ponders came quickly in "real time," fitting in many with just the blink of an eye, yet I find it amazing to receive them in what felt like "slow motion." I am thinking this is true "Godspeed."

Finding uninterrupted, true "stillness" can be hard. Even as Barry found a spot where the sunrise was beautiful… I could see tiny twinkling headlights of cars far in the distance. They made brakes in my stillness. He generously continued on and found a spot that was not as beautiful, but stillness was found.

In those moment I realized God is not slow, but I certainly am. God is not in a hurry, but I certainly am, and stillness trumps beauty…

It was in those moments I found true stillness. Godspeed time that I allowed myself to be exactly the person God created me to be. A human not fixated on who I am or what I want, but who the Lord is and what He wants…a powerful moment, and I was changed…at least for those moments, and in those moments I certainly sat in the fullness of the Glory of God.

Godspeed.

I shall ponder…

Appliances

n., devices or pieces of equipment designed to perform a specific task, typically a domestic one.

When we moved into our home…we determined an electric stove just wouldn't do. So we had a guy come out and run a gas line to the kitchen so we could replace the electric stove with a gas one. I have to say… I do love me a good gas stove.

The house also didn't have a microwave. How could this be? Apparently, the space used by the hood is too close to the stove. We had *no idea* how tied to a microwave we were! After much research I found a "low profile" model that is much shorter and meets the required eighteen-inch distance from the bottom of the microwave to the top of the stove.

Just as we were getting back into the swing of cooking/baking… we noticed ourselves rewashing all the dishes because the dishwasher wasn't getting them all clean. Turns out the dishwasher only has one wand under the bottom rack…requiring we only use the bottom rack for all dishes/pans that need to be "clean."

As my prayer partner says, "First world problems."

The word "hedonism" comes to mind "the pursuit of pleasure and/or self-indulgence."

Quite the ponder for a Christian heart…

After pondering… The Theology of Sandi believes that God created me with the desire to pursue pleasure…without that desire… I wouldn't have the longing/desire needed to pursue Himself. The problem comes when I, as a Christian, pursue self-indulgence.

"Biblical self-indulgence is feeding 'the passions of the flesh' (1 Pet. 2:11). It's indulging ourselves in any pleasure that is harmful to our souls, that does not spring from faith (Rom. 14:23)" (Jon Bloom).

Faith is not required to know that I can live in this "first world" God has placed me in…with an electric stove, a bottom of the line dishwasher and without a microwave. I have to ask myself, is seeking "better" pleasure or self-indulgence? Definitely a case-by-case situation.

Sometimes I forget that God wants me to be happy…instead of cautiously resisting it. But what God wants most…is for me to know that the most enduring happiness is found only in Him.

I shall ponder…

Yellow Rose

Conveys warmth and affection and can symbolize a warm memory or a token of appreciation to another.

I am "move-in" tired. After I make what seems like a three-mile trek down the hallway to get my morning coffee… I lay my head back on my ohhh so comfy "prayer chair" recliner to "hear" from God. All that can be heard are my snores of restfulness.

I worked hard at finding our possessions their new "place" and have been joyously working hard to begin the first strokes of my art yard. *Much* work is needed to prepare my canvas.

There are eight huge, old, overgrown rose bushes along the back fence. I try to prune one down every day or so. When I do…it is like a meet and greet of sorts.

The red rose had potential, fragrance and was kind to me as I cut her hair.

The pink rose was beautiful, without fragrance and absolutely unruly in character. She left many painful teeth marks as I tried to cut her hair and remove her sucker branches. She will not be living with us much longer.

The yellow rose… At first glance she looked like another wild one. Very old, very overgrown, and only a showing of a few small, feeble, yellow roses. As soon as I began to work with her…the fragrance of those few yellow roses were overwhelming and beautiful. I knew immediately we were going to be friends. I introduced myself—also old, overgrown, and needing a lot of work. I assured her she not only had a place in my art yard, but would be one of my focal points.

The truth is, we will help each other realize our beauty, as a focal point in God's yard art.

"I praise you, for I am fearfully and wonderfully made. Wonderful are your works; my soul knows it very well" (Ps. 139:14).

I shall ponder…

Perception vs. Perspective

Perception: *n.*, an interpretation that an individual comes up with through their awareness and can be influenced by past experiences, feelings, and thoughts.

Perspective: *n.*, a point of view, a framework we use to look at something and is more likely to be influenced by attitude.

Yesterday, I began a ponder on perception, or was it perspective? I can't remember and I wasn't sure of the difference.

It seems...my interpretations (perceptions) lead me to a point of view (perspective).

Does this matter?

I suppose so, or the psychosocial peeps of this world wouldn't have written such extensive information about it. But I must ponder how this information relates to me.

Pride comes to mind.

While pride causes me to filter out any perception of nastiness I see in myself...it also causes me to filter out God's goodness in others. My pride allows their faults to create a "perception" about them and eventually a "perspective" of who they are...viewing them through developed attitudes...possibly words of nastiness...written around the framework I view them through.

Grace on the other hand...is undeserved favor.

Grace causes me to see God in myself and others. It causes me to filter out nastiness, faults, developed attitudes, and undeserved perceptions and perspectives.

My ponder leads me to this personal statement; "Perception vs. perspective doesn't matter when looking through the framework of grace."

There is more to this, so I shall ponder...

Virtual Reality

n., a reality that is only based in the computer.

Yesterday our streets were repaved. A nice "welcome to the neighborhood" gift from the city of Vacaville. I spent the day listening for the beeping of equipment passing by so I could video the layers of repaving excitement to my great nephew who loves himself some large moving equipment.

My brother-in-law in Jersey is a large equipment operator. I so wish I could arrange for John T and Charlie to meet for a ride on one of his pieces of road equipment...way better than a video!

Virtual never replaces reality, but it can be a tool.

FaceTime has helped me create and sustain a relationship with my niece-lette in Indiana. I can watch her grow. Learn the expressions on her face...that speak volumes. That girl is a character. She's learning I am one too!

The Marco Polo app has kept the Cali family up to date on day-to-day news...what's cooking in the kitchen and trivialities such as "fly away hairs" the Hall women seem to be dealing with. The greatest moments have been when no words were spoken but when a "look," nod, or shaking of the head said it all.

The thing is, while a helpful tool, FaceTime did not teach my niece-lette she could trust her whacky great aunt; it was "time" given when we visited their home in Indiana last spring. She "experienced" my directness, my consistency. She felt my unrelenting love in a cuddle. She learned she could trust me, not just by how I interacted with her, but also how I interacted with others.

I wonder if God sees me in a virtual sense, when I am "doing church," instead of "being the church," when I tell God what is going on in my life and how I want it fixed, instead of offering him a wordless nod of faith.

I am certain God sees me in reality, when trust is developed between us through experience and consistency. When consistency is displayed not only by how I interact with Him, but how I interact with others. When I allow myself to be vulnerable enough to receive His unrelenting love in a cuddle, even when I don't like the choice he has just made for me.

I shall ponder…

A New Human

Last night I met my new granddaughter.

A new human being weighing seven pounds, three ounces, named Liberty Jean.

A new human being with black curly hair and currently undetermined eye color.

A new human being not randomly, but divinely placed into her parents' arms.

A new human being placed on this earth with potential, purpose, and grace.

A new human being who will be taught "*in the way that [she] should go,*" while still being given the freedom to "go" wherever God takes her.

A new human being that makes her grandpa's chin quiver with emotion and her grandma's heart quiver with prayer.

A new human being whose grandparents' greatest gifts will not be toys or technology, but time, relationship, and example.

Last night, I met my new granddaughter, and she is perfect.

I shall ponder…

About the Author

Sandi Hall, writer, artist, Christian, prayer warrior who rises very early every morning to spend quality time with the Lord, in study, prayer, and ponderings. She is more comfortable sharing her weaknesses than her strengths.

A season of Sandi's humorous, honest, real, and often deep ponderings were penned during a portion of the now infamous year, "2020." This book is a collection of those ponderings.

Sandi lives in Central California with her husband, Barry, and her two dogs, Franklyn Bell and Harriet Bean.

To learn more visit sunriseponders.com or follow Sandi on Instagram at SunrisePonders

CPSIA information can be obtained
at www.ICGtesting.com
Printed in the USA
BVHW021438050422
633416BV00009B/284

9 781639 030569